→ The role of genetics in aggression is also supported by research by Brunner (1993) in a large family from the Netherlands whose members were displaying high levels of [violence], arson, and impulsive aggression. Five of the males were found to have the dysfunctional [MAOA gene, which] suggests that this genetic fault is the cause of their aggression. However, this study [shows] differences in how a dysfunctional MAOA gene affects behaviour. The females in the [family did not show genetic] dysfunction. The MAOA gene is carried on the X chromosome, and as females have [two X chromosomes, if they] possess the dysfunctional MAOA gene, their corresponding X chromosome is likely [to have a functional MAOA gene, which] has been found to be dominant. This means that when investigating aggression and genetics, research should consider the impact of gender differences too.

→ One limitation of the genetic explanation of aggression is that there is no acknowledgement of the role of social and environmental factors. For example, someone may become aggressive because of financial pressures or in response to stressors rather than because of a genetic dysfunction. This means that whilst the genetic explanation offers a scientific approach to understanding aggression and is compatible with the aims of science, it does not include the role that our nurture/experiences can have on our behaviours. However, it may be more suitable to take a diathesis-stress / interactionist approach to explain aggression. For example, someone may have a genetic vulnerability to aggression that is only triggered when a stressor or trauma is experienced. This is a better alternative to genetic theories since it acknowledges the role of both nature and nurture.

→ One limitation of the genetic explanation is that there are too many anomalies. Whilst many aggressive people have been found to have a chromosomal or other genetic difference, there are plenty of people who do not. In addition, some people with genetic dysfunction have not gone on to display aggressive behaviours. This means that, at best, the genetic explanation of aggression can only explain why some of the general population are aggressive, which indicates that the genetic explanation is either inaccurate or needs to be offered in collaboration with another theory.

Issues and Debates

→ One limitation of the genetic explanation is that it is criticised for being biologically reductionist. This means that it reduces a complex trait like aggression down to the lowest level of explanation, choosing to focus on genetics at the expense of other influences such as neuroanatomy, stress or relationships. This is a limitation because there are several factors that influence our behaviour, and different people are also likely to be aggressive for different reasons. This means that an explanation of aggression needs to acknowledge how complex the trait is and avoid breaking it down into just one testable cause.

→ However, being biologically reductionist is not always a limitation. The genetic explanation has been able to isolate one gene that could be contributing to aggression, and therefore this can be used to implement interventions to reduce aggression. Without a reductionist approach to investigating aggression, these interventions would not exist.

→ One limitation of the genetic explanation is that it is criticised for being socially sensitive. This is because the assumption that aggression is determined by our genetics is not compatible with our legal system. The law expects that people take responsibility for their behaviour and make prosocial choices, not antisocial ones. If the genetic explanation was taken at face value, it would mean that people could not be held accountable for their behaviour and, therefore, not deserving of custodial sentences and other interventions.

Possible Exam Questions

1. Which one of the following refers to aggression? (1 mark)
   a) Prosocial behaviour
   b) Avoidant behaviour
   c) Insecure behaviour
   d) Antisocial behaviour

2. Outline the role of chromosomes in aggression. (2 marks)
   Exam Hint: For this question, you only need a little bit of elaboration, and you must keep focused on aggression.

3. Outline the role of one gene that is implicated in aggression (e.g. MAOA gene). (3 marks)
   Exam Hint: Here, you would have XYY and MAOA to choose between, so think carefully about which one you can outline in more detail and which one will allow you to demonstrate the most understanding. For three marks, the answer needs detail, terminology and some elaboration.

4. Explain how twin studies can be used to investigate the role of genetics in aggression. (4 marks)
Exam Hint: For this question, make sure you focus on twin studies and not adoption or general family studies. Ideally, you will explain concordance rates and be able to explain HOW twins are studied. Note that the question is not asking you to talk about a specific study.

5. Explain the reductionism and holism debate. Refer to aggression in your answer. (6 marks)
Exam Hint: There are two tasks to complete here. Firstly, you need to ensure that you explain the debate, and secondly, you need to make sure that your answer is applied to aggression. Don't forget that since this is a 'debate', you must refer to both reductionism and holism in your answer.

6. Brenda and Bob run a café together. Recently, Brenda has started to be aggressive towards Bob. For example, she has been verbally insulting him and has started to control where he can and cannot go after work. Bob confides in his friend, who advises him to leave and seek professional support. Bob says that it is not Brenda's fault since her mother was the same when she was her age. Outline the genetic explanation of aggression and refer to the scenario in your answer. (6 marks)
Exam Hint: For this question, you will need to give an outline of the role of genetics and then weave in some application to Bob. Spot the reference to genetics and use it to frame your answer.

7. A newspaper article claims that people are not responsible for their behaviours when they are aggressive during arguments since they are genetically preprogrammed to react this way if they have aggressive parents. Readers are complaining that this suggests criminals are not to blame for their behaviour. Explain why the genetic explanation of aggression can be criticised for being socially sensitive. Refer to the scenario in your answer. (4 marks)
Exam Hint: Although you do need to spend time talking about the issue of social sensitivity, you need to make sure that your answer is focused on aggression throughout. You may choose to refer to the article proposal or the audience response, or you may choose to incorporate both. Avoid the temptation to merely repeat what has already been said in the scenario.

8. Discuss the role of genetics in aggression. (8 marks)
Exam Hint: Make sure you think about what the command word 'discuss' means so that you are able to satisfy the marking criteria. The question is an extended writing one, but it is only worth eight marks, so you do need to make sure you select the evaluation points that you want to use for discussion by thinking ahead. Don't forget to include some knowledge.

9. Explain one strength of the genetic explanation of schizophrenia. (4 marks)
Exam Hint: Choose one strength that you know you can elaborate on, especially since there are four marks to earn here, and you must do that by showing your knowledge and understanding, as well as developing some good discussion.

10. Outline and evaluate the genetic explanation of aggression. (16 marks)
Exam Hint: Whilst you must ensure that you offer a detailed and knowledgeable account of the theory, remember that most marks in this question are for effective evaluation. Choose research to support and challenge the theory, but be sure to stay focused on the explanation.

AQA A LEVEL PSYCHOLOGY

EXAM BUSTER

Aggression

tutor2u

www.tutor2u.net

BIOLOGICAL EXPLANATIONS OF AGGRESSION: GENETICS

Specification: Neural and hormonal mechanisms in aggression, including the roles of the limbic system, serotonin and testosterone. Genetic factors in aggression, including the MAOA gene.

WHAT YOU NEED TO KNOW
➡ The role of genetics in aggressive behaviour, including the MAOA gene.
➡ Research to support/challenge the role of genetics in aggression.
➡ Strengths and limitations of genetics and biological explanations of aggression.

Aggression refers to a range of behaviours that can result in both physical and psychological harm to oneself, other people, or objects in the environment. The expression of aggression can occur in several ways, including physically, verbally, mentally, and emotionally. Psychologists also distinguish between two different types of aggression: impulsive aggression (typically unplanned and characterised by strong emotions, normally anger); and instrumental aggression (usually carefully planned with the intention of achieving a goal). Here, we will look at the role of genetics in aggression as one of the main biological explanations you need to know.

The Role of Genetics in Aggression

According to the biological explanation of aggression, genetics play a crucial part, and geneticists assume that it is a hereditary behaviour. For example, whilst biological males have the XY sex chromosomes, and biological females have the XX sex chromosomes, some people have an XYY combination. Those with this genetic combination would be male, but the additional Y chromosome would lead to an increase in testosterone production. This pattern has been called the 'warrior gene' since the additional Y chromosome has been linked to the increase in aggression found in those with this chromosomal pattern.

Geneticists have also investigated aggression amongst twins, expecting that there would be higher concordance amongst monozygotic twins (identical) than dizygotic twins (non-identical). Since monozygotic twins are 100% genetically identical in contrast to non-identical twins, the higher concordance rates would support the role of genes in aggression.

The **MAOA** gene has been identified as significant when it comes to aggression. The gene is responsible for the production of MAOA (Monoamine Oxidase A), which is a protein that helps to break down excess neurotransmitters in synapses within the brain. Usually, this protein helps the reuptake process in synaptic transmission, ensuring that there are regulated amounts of **serotonin**, dopamine, and noradrenaline in the brain. When the MAOA gene is faulty or dysfunctional, this prevents neurotransmitters from being broken down. This would lead to an imbalance of chemicals such as serotonin and dopamine, which would then cause aggression. For example, high levels of dopamine are linked to aggression, and low levels of serotonin (which usually helps us to feel calm) are also linked to aggression.

Evaluating The Role of Genetics on Aggression

➡ One strength of the genetic explanation of aggression is that there is a wealth of research evidence in support of the theory. Godar et al. (2014) used selective breeding to remove the MAOA gene in mice, to see what effect this would have on their behaviour. The mice became more aggressive, and they had disrupted levels of serotonin. They also found that when the mice were given medication to help balance their serotonin levels, the aggressive behaviour stopped. This supports the role of genetics in aggression and the influence that genetics can have on neurotransmitters.

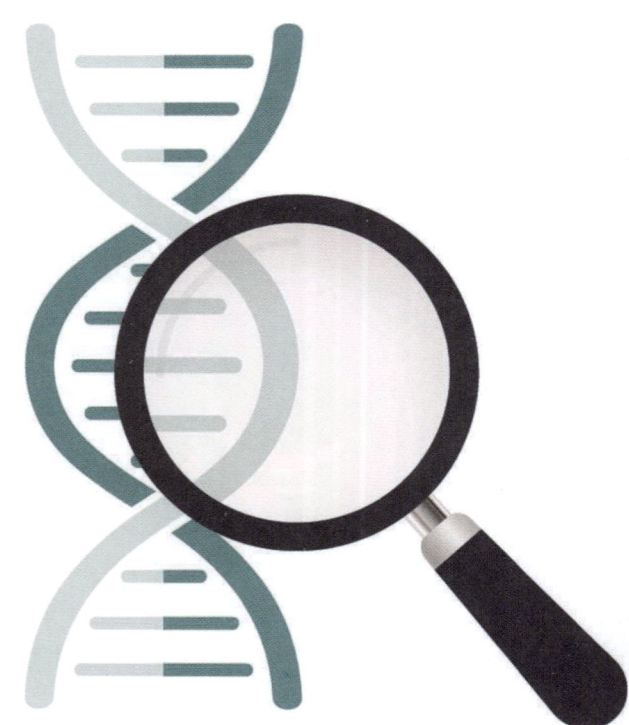

➡ However, there are extrapolation issues with research on animals that affect how well results and conclusions can be generalised to humans. For example, the aggression that humans demonstrate is both psychological and physical, and since this distinction cannot be made in an animal sample, the results lack the validity needed to help us learn about why humans become aggressive and what we can do to reduce aggression.

BIOLOGICAL EXPLANATIONS OF AGGRESSION: NEURAL & HORMONAL EXPLANATIONS

Specification: Neural and hormonal mechanisms in aggression, including the roles of the limbic system, serotonin and testosterone. Genetic factors in aggression, including the MAOA gene.

WHAT YOU NEED TO KNOW
➡ How hormones contribute to aggression.
➡ The role of different neurotransmitters and brain structures in aggressive behaviour.
➡ Evaluation of the neural and hormonal explanation of aggression.

Neural and Hormonal Explanations of Aggression

This explanation of aggression focuses on the role of neuroanatomy, neurotransmitters, and hormones, suggesting that if there is dysfunction or underdevelopment in these areas of an individual, aggression is likely to occur.

The **limbic system** is offered as a **neural** explanation, suggesting that brain structures in the limbic system such as the amygdala, hypothalamus, and hippocampus are all implicated in aggression. The limbic system has physical connections to the prefrontal cortex, which is involved in forward planning and reward anticipation, so if there is a problem with the structure of the prefrontal cortex, this could result in reactive aggression. In addition, structural issues in the limbic system affect the way we respond to situations and perceived threats, suggesting that neuroanatomical structure is significant in aggression.

The hypothalamus is another brain region that is implicated in aggression. This part of the brain is responsible for the regulation of the autonomic nervous system, which helps us determine our emotional responses to situations or perceived threats. Therefore, damage to the hypothalamus is one reason why someone may become aggressive.

In addition to neural explanations, hormones and neurotransmitters also play a part in aggression. For example, serotonin is a neurotransmitter that helps us to feel calm, so when the levels of this chemical are depleted or too low, this prevents someone from controlling their aggressive behaviour and impulsivity. Serotonin is also implicated in the normal functioning of the prefrontal cortex, helping to regulate our response to external stimuli. Those who have abnormal levels of serotonin will therefore struggle to anticipate risk appropriately, leading to risk-taking behaviours, including aggression.

Finally, **testosterone** is one hormone that appears to be implicated in aggression. Research tends to find that men are more aggressive than females, and since men have higher levels of testosterone, this hormone is assumed to be significant in aggression.

Evaluating Neural and Hormonal Explanations of Aggression

- One strength of this explanation of aggression is that there is research support. Kluver and Bucy (1939) removed parts of the limbic system in Rhesus monkeys (such as the amygdala). They found that the monkeys started to demonstrate an absence of emotion and fear, even in response to stimuli that they would normally fear. Some of the monkeys also appeared to lose understanding of group hierarchies and were aggressive towards the more dominant monkeys in the group. This suggests that the limbic system is important in regulating our aggressive impulses and behaviours and that impairments may be the reason why some people are aggressive.

- Another strength of this explanation is that it is able to investigate aggression in a way that is compatible with the aims of science. For example, Wong et al. (1997) used MRI scans to investigate neural structures such as the amygdala and found that violent male criminals in Broadmoor hospital had a smaller amygdala than a control group. This suggests that the brain is

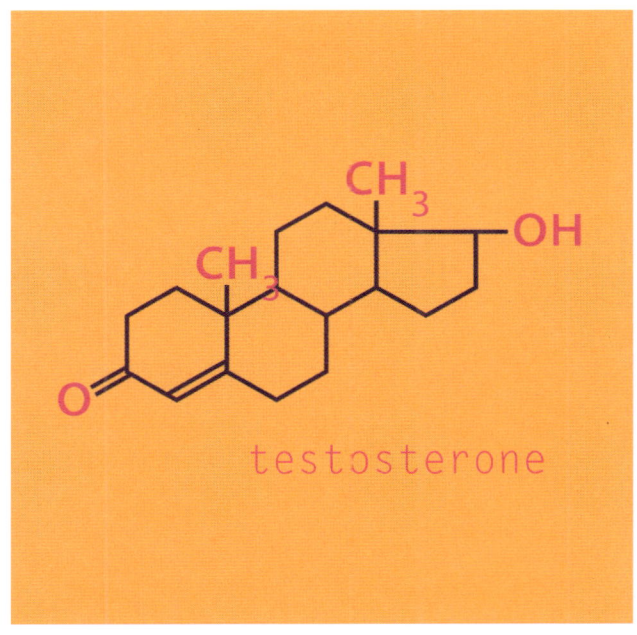

influential in aggression and demonstrates the objective and testable way that this explanation demonstrates a link between the brain and aggression.

⇨ One limitation of this explanation is that many argue it is bidirectional. For example, whilst Raine et al. (1997) found that murderers had reduced activity in the prefrontal cortex compared to non-murderers, cause and effect cannot be established. Similarly, if an aggressive person has high levels of testosterone, cause and effect cannot be established here either. This is because whilst the brain and hormones/neurotransmitters may lead to aggression, they may also be affected by the aggression. In other words, it is not possible to know whether the biological abnormalities precede or follow aggression.

⇨ A final strength of this explanation is that it has led to various interventions for helping people with aggression. For example, some people with extremely high levels of testosterone can be treated with hormone therapy to help reduce their aggression. In addition, it is also possible to have a surgery called an 'amygdalotomy' where the amygdala is disconnected from the rest of the brain. People who have this surgery experience a loss of emotion, but this includes a loss of aggression. These interventions suggest that this explanation of aggression has been able to contribute to the prevention and reduction of aggression, which may also positively affect crime rates.

Issues and Debates

⇨ One limitation of this explanation of aggression is that it could be considered gender-biased. Many of the studies used to support it are only conducted on male samples. This is beta bias and assumes that the findings from male samples can also be used to explain female aggression and behaviours. This is a limitation because it minimises the differences between men and women and fails to acknowledge differences that would matter. For example, women have higher levels of the hormone oxytocin which means they respond to stress and threats in a very different way than males. Just this one **hormonal** difference alone suggests that men cannot represent women in aggression research.

⇨ Another limitation of the explanation is that it is criticised for being biologically deterministic. This means that the explanation assumes that aggression is the result of biological factors that are beyond an individual's control. This is a limitation since it does not acknowledge the role of free will and choice that people have in how they behave. A deterministic view like this suggests that people who are aggressive are not responsible for their behaviour, and this could create problems for society and justice.

Possible Exam Questions

1. Which one of the following is an example of a hormone? (1 mark)
    a) Amygdala
    b) Testosterone
    c) Serotonin
    d) Hippocampus

2. Outline the role of hormones in aggression. (2 marks)
Exam Hint: For this question, you only need some elaboration, and you must keep focused on aggression. Make sure you select an appropriate hormone rather than a neurotransmitter.

3. Outline the role of the brain in aggression. (3 marks)
Exam Hint: For three marks, you will not be able to talk about everything that is covered in this chapter. You should select one example of brain dysfunction and explain how it contributes to aggression.

4. Summarise findings of research that support the neural and hormonal explanation of aggression. (4 marks)
Exam Hint: For this question, you should only focus on the 'findings', so since you are not able to use procedures, you should be prepared to talk about more than one study. Remember to talk about how it supports the explanation.

5. Explain one limitation of the neural and hormonal explanation of aggression. (4 marks)
Exam Hint: For four marks, you will need to elaborate on your point. This is a good opportunity for you to use terminology, keep your work structured and show examiners that you understand the limitation you have selected to offer. You do not need to counter the point – stay focused on the limitation.

6. Cassandra is trying to do her homework, but she is distracted by her siblings. Her brother, Robert, tends to play more aggressive games with his friends, punching and shouting at each other. On the other hand, her sister, Genie, avoids

confrontation and aggression with other people. Using your knowledge of aggression, explain why there might be a difference in the behaviour of Cassandra's siblings. (4 marks)

Exam Hint: Read the scenario carefully and make sure you can distinguish between Robert and Genie's behaviour. Avoid the temptation of regurgitating information from the scenario, and instead, ensure your answer is framed around aggression and a possible gender difference such as hormones.

7. Discuss the neural and hormonal explanation of aggression. (8 marks)

Exam Hint: It won't be possible for you to talk about everything here, so you need to be selective. Don't forget that you should also offer more evaluation than knowledge. If you opt to use your knowledge of issues and debates, make sure you make it relevant to aggression to make it effective.

8. Outline and evaluate the neural and hormonal explanation of aggression. (16 marks)

Exam Hint: Typically, you should spend 20-25 minutes on a question like this, and remember that most of it should be demonstrating your skill of evaluation. You can compare and contrast other theories of aggression, but always keep focused on the theory named in the question

SOCIAL PSYCHOLOGICAL EXPLANATIONS OF HUMAN AGGRESSION: DEINDIVIDUATION

Specification: Social psychological explanations of human aggression: including frustration-aggression hypothesis, Social learning theory as applied to human aggression, and deindividuation.

WHAT YOU NEED TO KNOW
⇒ Explain how deindividuated behaviour differs from individual behaviour.
⇒ Summarise how deindividuation occurs and why it leads to aggression.
⇒ Evaluate the deindividuation explanation of aggression.

Explaining Deindividuation Theory

Deindividuation is a psychological state that people enter once they are in a situation that leads to the loss of their personal identity. For example, individuals may assume the identity of a social group, a uniform or a disguise. This puts them into a deindividuated state and prevents them from being able to self-regulate their behaviour, leading to an increased risk of behaving aggressively.

Le Bon (1895) suggested that crowds are likely to lead to deindividuation because individuals do not stand out and are not easily identifiable. With the anonymity to behave how they please and the freedom from social constraints of behaviour, individuals may behave in ways they would not normally, such as being aggressive (physical or verbal) towards others. Le Bon claims that being in a crowd leads to the diffusion of responsibility for any consequences or blame that might occur for their behaviour, and this leads to less guilt and less remorse about anti-social behaviour.

Zimbardo (1969) also suggests that darkness, distance and drugs are also factors that can lead to this deindividuated state and highlights that deindividuated behaviours are impulsive, irrational and emotional; this is what increases the likelihood of someone behaving aggressively. For example, football hooligans may attend a football match (crowd) and wear the team kit (uniform), and these both contribute to feelings of anonymity, increasing the likelihood that someone will behave aggressively towards others or chant inappropriate and offensive songs – regardless of whether they would do this in their normal day to day life.

In addition to this, Dunn and Rogers (1982) highlight two specific reasons why people become deindividuated by crowds, uniforms, and other influences.

⇒ Private self-awareness is inhibited: usually, we are self-aware about our behaviours and whether they are appropriate or not, but this is not the case in the deindividuated state.

⇒ Public self-awareness is inhibited: usually, we care what other people think about us and our behaviours, but this is not the case in the deindividuated state.

Evaluating Deindividuation Theory

⇒ One strength of this explanation of aggression is that there are positive implications that derive from it. For example, strategies can be used to reduce the effect of deindividuation, such as mirrors and increased CCTV at group events (e.g. sports). Furthermore, research has also found that there is a strong correlation between sending threatening/hostile messages online and anonymity (e.g. hiding your real identity).

- One strength of this explanation is that it can have a positive impact on the economy. For example, if implications such as increased CCTV, an increased presence of police, and changes to social media legislation were to be brought in, then this would reduce crime rates and improve mental wellbeing, thus reducing the cost of dealing with offenders.

- One strength of this explanation is that there is research to support the link between aggression and deindividuation. Dodd (1985) asked 229 undergraduate psychology students: 'if you could do anything humanly possible with complete assurance that you would not be detected or held responsible, what would you do?'. Three independent raters scored the students' responses into those that were antisocial and those that were not. The results found that 36% of the responses were antisocial and 26% were criminal (types of responses referring to acts such as 'robbing a bank'). This research demonstrates the connection between deindividuation as a result of anonymity and subsequent aggression.

- One limitation of this explanation is that research does not always support a link between deindividuation and aggression. Gerges et al. (1973) found that when eight strangers were placed in a dark room together for an hour with no rules to follow and told that they would never see each other again, it did not take long for talking to cease and for kissing each other to start. In another study, they were told that they would see each again, and this time they did not kiss each other. However, aggression was not demonstrated in either study, suggesting that deindividuation does not inevitably lead to aggression.

Issues and Debates

- One limitation of this explanation of aggression is that it could be considered socially sensitive. This is because the assumption that all crowds and all uniforms will lead to aggression is not entirely accurate but could lead to serious implications. Johnson and Downing (1979) found that when participants were asked to give electric shocks to a confederate, they were less likely to give them shocks if they were dressed as a nurse (a prosocial uniform) and more likely to give shocks if they were dressed in a KKK (Klu Klux Klan) uniform. This suggests that aggression is largely dependent on the type of uniform someone wears or the type of crowd that they are in.

- One limitation of this explanation is that it is environmentally reductionist. This is because it assumes that aggression can be explained with just one level of explanation (situation) and disregards the notion that aggression is a continuum of behaviour and can occur for multiple reasons. A more holistic approach to explaining aggression would be more suitable since this would allow pre-natal influences, socio economic pressures and other experiences to be taken into consideration in addition to deindividuation.

Possible Exam Questions

1. Which one of the following refers to deindividuation? (1 mark)
   a) Psychological state
   b) Sociological state
   c) Aggressive state
   d) Economic state

2. Outline what is meant by the term 'deindividuation'. (2 marks)
Exam Hint: For this question, you only need some elaboration, and you must keep focused on aggression.

3. Outline the role of deindividuation in aggression. (4 marks)
Exam Hint: Here, you should be selective with what you choose to talk about. You do not need to talk about every example or reason why someone may enter a deindividuated state. Do make sure you have explicit links to aggression.

4. Explain how crowds may lead to aggressive behaviour according to the deindividuation explanation of aggression. (4 marks)
Exam Hint: For this question, make sure you focus on aggression and avoid being too general in your answer. Whilst you should focus on crowds as opposed to uniforms, you should explain the psychology behind why a crowd would lead to deindividuation.

5. Summarise findings of research into deindividuation. (6 marks)
Exam Hint: Notice that the question is only asking you to talk about the findings of the research, so you will need to focus on the results of the studies and avoid being distracted by the procedures or methodological details.

6. Javid works as a solicitor during the week and enjoys going to watch rugby matches with his friends. During the matches, he feels exhilarated standing amongst all of the team fans and sings along with their chants, even if they are offensive to the opposition players or fans. Use your knowledge of Javid to explain why Javid may be experiencing deindividuation. (6 marks)

Exam Hint: You should spot here that Javid has a respectable professional that is not normally associated with aggression and inappropriate behaviour. Use this to explain the changes in Javid and use theoretical knowledge to explain why they occur.

7. A local politician is campaigning to change entry policies into nightclubs. She wants everyone who enters a nightclub to have their passport scanned and to be issued with a personal reference number, visible to security officers and CCTV. Young people in the area are not happy with this proposal and do not understand why this is needed. Use your knowledge of deindividuation to explain the purpose of the suggestions from the politician. (4 marks)

Exam Hint: In this question, you need to demonstrate your knowledge of the theory whilst justifying why the politician has reached the conclusion that these suggested changes would be a good idea. Consider the location of a nightclub and how that might be a plan where aggression occurs.

8. Discuss deindividuation as an explanation for human aggression. (8 marks)

Exam Hint: Make sure you think about what the command word 'discuss' means so that you are able to satisfy the marking criteria. The question is an extended writing one, but it is only worth eight marks, so you do need to make sure you select the evaluation points that you want to use for discussion by thinking ahead. Don't forget to include some knowledge.

9. Evaluate the deindividuation explanation of aggression. (4 marks)

Exam Hint: For this evaluation question, you can choose to focus on negative criticism, positive, or both. You are also not limited to just one; however, take note of how many marks this question is worth to give you an idea of how long to spend on it.

10. Outline and evaluate the deindividuation explanation of aggression. (16 marks)

Exam Hint: Whilst you must ensure that you offer a detailed and knowledgeable account of the theory, remember that most marks in this question are for effective evaluation. Choose research to support and challenge the theory, but be sure to stay focused on the explanation.

SOCIAL PSYCHOLOGICAL EXPLANATIONS OF HUMAN AGGRESSION: FRUSTRATION AGGRESSION HYPOTHESIS

Specification: Social psychological explanations of human aggression: including frustration-aggression hypothesis, Social learning theory as applied to human aggression, and deindividuation.

WHAT YOU NEED TO KNOW
⇨ Outline of the frustration-aggression hypothesis.
⇨ Research to support/challenge the frustration-aggression hypothesis.
⇨ Evaluate the frustration-aggression hypothesis.

There are many explanations of aggression that do not focus on the evolution or biological influences on behaviour, such as social psychological theories. One such social psychological theory is the frustration-aggression hypothesis.

Explaining the Frustration–Aggression Hypothesis

Dollard et al. (1939) proposed that when anyone experiences a feeling of **frustration**, this will inevitably lead to aggression, and that aggression is always the result of the frustration. This is the foundation of the frustration-aggression hypothesis and is based on psychodynamic assumptions about 'catharsis'. According to the psychodynamic approach, we have innate drives that need to be relieved or satisfied (such as anger), and there are two defence mechanisms that may be implicated in aggression.

- ⇨ **Sublimation** – engaging in activities or sports that provide an appropriate and safe way to vent your frustration
- ⇨ **Displacement** – re-directing your frustration and anger towards something or someone else

According to this hypothesis, aggression is more likely to occur when the individual who is experiencing the frustration is unable to resolve it. For example, if there is a barrier to completing a goal or implementing a solution, then the frustration drive cannot be satisfied, and aggression is the outcome. This aggression may be direct or indirect, and it could also be psychological or physical aggression.

Dollard et al. (1939) suggest reasons why some aggression may be indirect:
- ⇨ The frustration is caused by someone or something that is abstract (e.g. government)
- ⇨ There is a fear of consequences that prevent direct aggression (e.g. police)
- ⇨ The object of the frustration may not be available (e.g. you may not see your colleague until the next day and therefore cannot act on your frustration)

Evaluating the Frustration – Aggression Hypothesis

- ⇨ One limitation of the frustration-aggression hypothesis is that there is no acknowledgement of other variables that may contribute to the aggression. For example, not everyone who experiences frustration will become aggressive, and not everyone who acts aggressively has done so because of frustration. Berkowitz and Le Page (1967) found that participants behaved more aggressively (delivering electric shocks to others) when they were in the presence of weapons, showing that environmental cues must play a part.

- ⇨ One strength of the frustration-aggression hypothesis is that there is research to support it. Geen (1968) conducted a laboratory experiment where he asked male undergraduate students to undertake a jigsaw puzzle in one of three conditions

that had varying levels of frustration. One condition imposed an unattainable time limit to complete the jigsaw; in another condition, the jigsaw was impossible to complete; and in a third condition, a confederate issued derogatory remarks to the students as they failed to complete the study. Following this, participants had the opportunity to give shocks to the confederate if he answered incorrectly on another task. The group of participants who had experienced insults from the confederate gave the highest levels of shocks. All three groups gave more shocks than the control group that had not experienced any frustration. This experiment supports the theory that frustration leads to aggression.

➡ One limitation of this explanation of aggression is that catharsis can often be a counterproductive rather than a helpful way to defend against aggressive behaviour. For example, Bushman (2002) concluded that people get angrier the more that they hit a punch bag, suggesting that engaging in the sublimation of frustration can increase the likelihood of behaving or thinking aggressively. This is a limitation because the frustration-aggression hypothesis does not make this distinction.

➡ Another limitation of this explanation is that frustration may not be the only precursor to aggression, and it is recognised that other emotions can lead to aggression. For example, jealousy and pain can cause people to become aggressive, with feelings of frustration absent. In addition, some people may become determined rather than aggressive, following frustration. This led Berkowitz (1989) to reimagine the frustration-aggression hypothesis and offer the 'negative effect theory' as a more holistic alternative.

Issues and Debates

➡ One limitation of this explanation of human aggression is that it can be criticised for being a socially sensitive theory which could have implications for political and legislative change. For example, the gun control discussions and legislation in the USA may have to consider the notion that the availability of guns increases the likelihood that someone who is frustrated may turn to violence and, therefore, could impact their economy and amendment rights.

➡ One limitation of the frustration-aggression theory is that it could be considered environmentally reductionist. This is because the explanation focuses on the impact of external cues, stressors and barriers as an explanation of aggression, at the expense of acknowledging a wider, more holistic range of influences such as hormones and neural activity.

Possible Exam Questions

1. Which one of the following refers to the frustration-aggression hypothesis? (1 mark)
    a) Reactive aggression
    b) Proactive aggression
    c) Prosocial behaviour
    d) Evolutionary behaviour

2. Outline the frustration-aggression hypothesis. (4 marks)
Exam Hint: For this question, you do not need to give an overly detailed account of the theory, but you do need to elaborate to demonstrate your understanding of it.

3. Explain what is meant by 'catharsis' in the context of the frustration-aggression hypothesis. (3 marks)
Exam Hint: You should offer some elaboration here – do not just define catharsis. You could give an example (e.g. sublimation) but always come back to the question and remain focused.

4. Explain one limitation of the frustration-aggression hypothesis. (4 marks)
Exam Hint: For this question, choose only one point to talk about and make sure it is a negative criticism. Offer some elaborate and keep it structured.

5. Explain one strength of the frustration-aggression hypothesis. (4 marks)
Exam Hint: For this question, choose only one point to talk about and make sure it is a positive criticism. If you choose to use research support, keep focused on the actual theory instead of talking too much about the study.

6. Assess the frustration-aggression hypothesis. (6 marks)
Exam Hint: This question is only assessing evaluation, so there are no command words asking you to talk about the actual theory. Select two evaluation points to talk about (strength or limitations) and offer structure, terminology and elaborate.

7. Jack has been waiting in the car for his mum whilst she goes into the shop. It is a hot day and the car windows are up, and the door is centrally locked. Jack gets hotter and starts to feel very irritable and frustrated at how long his mum is taking. He

tries to wind the windows down and tries to fan himself with a piece of paper, but nothing is helping. He becomes so frustrated that he punches the dashboard.

Explain why Jack became aggressive in this situation, using your knowledge of the frustration-aggression hypothesis. (4 marks)

Exam Hint: This question allows you to demonstrate your knowledge of the theory whilst talking about Jack. Spend time thinking about what Jack was doing in the car and why the end result was aggression.

8. Laura is in a meeting with her colleagues, and they need to come to a decision urgently about an event happening later that day at work. Her colleagues are not focused and are spending too much time talking about an event happening the week after. Laura asks them to focus and stick to the agenda, but they soon go off-topic. Laura shows them how much time they have left to make a decision and explains the consequences of not reaching a decision. Although they are all listening to Laura, someone walks into the office and asks them to leave the room so the painting can be done. Laura shouts loudly at the team and walks off, kicking her locker as she walks past it.

Outline the frustration-aggression hypothesis. Refer to Laura in your answer. (8 marks)

Exam Hint: Note that this question is not asking you to evaluate the explanation, but you do need to demonstrate your knowledge and application skills. Spend time looking at the triggers that caused the aggressive behaviour and think about how you can relate this to the theory before you start writing your answer.

9. Outline and evaluate the frustration-aggression explanation of aggression. (16 marks)

Exam Hint: Whilst you must ensure that you offer a detailed and knowledgeable account of the theory, remember that most marks in this question are for effective evaluation. Choose research to support and challenge the theory, but be sure to stay focused on the explanation.

SOCIAL PSYCHOLOGICAL EXPLANATIONS OF HUMAN AGGRESSION: SLT AS APPLIED TO HUMAN AGGRESSION

Specification: Social psychological explanations of human aggression: including frustration-aggression hypothesis, Social learning theory as applied to human aggression, and deindividuation.

WHAT YOU NEED TO KNOW
➡ Apply social learning theory to human aggression.
➡ Outline strengths of the social learning theory of human aggression.
➡ Outline limitations of the social learning theory of human aggression.

Explaining The Social Learning Theory as Applied to Aggression

According to Bandura (1973), aggression is an observable behaviour that is learned through experience rather than solely the result of biological influences. According to **social learning theory**, aggression is learned through either direct or indirect experiences:

- ➡ **Direct learning:** an individual may learn behaviour based on their own experiences and the consequences of their actions. For example, if a child hits another child and is grounded, then this punishment weakens the likelihood of the behaviour (hitting) being repeated. However, if a child bullies another child and steals their money, then the bully may be positively reinforced (through financial gain) and repeat this behaviour again in the future.

- ➡ **Indirect learning:** an individual does not have to experience something themselves in order to learn aggression. Aggression is acquired through the observation of others and the outcomes of their behaviour. For example, if a young boy watches aggressive sports and sees the most aggressive player become a hero, then the young boy may imitate this behaviour because of vicarious learning.

SLT also acknowledges the cognitive influences and recognises that we are too complex to merely observe and imitate behaviours. According to SLT, there are a number of cognitive processes, including:

➡ **Attention**: A person/child must pay attention to the aggressor; for instance, when a child engages in a computer game or watches a violent film, they are attending to the aggression.

➡ **Retention**: To model the behaviour, it needs to be stored in long-term memory, which enables the behaviour to be retrieved. A child needs to remember the aggression that they have witnessed.

➡ **Reproduction**: The individual needs to be able to reproduce the behaviour, i.e. have the physical capabilities. If this is not the case, then the observed behaviour cannot be imitated.

➡ **Motivation**: An individual may expect to receive positive reinforcement for the modelled behaviour.

➡ **Self-efficacy**: Individuals must believe that their behaviour will attain a goal; they must have confidence in their own ability to carry out the action and that they will be rewarded for that action.

Evaluating The Social Learning Theory as Applied to Aggression

- One strength of the social learning theory of aggression is that it is supported by a wealth of empirical evidence. For example, Bandura (1963) conducted a study with three experimental conditions: in one condition, there was a filmed aggressive role model; in another condition, there was an aggressive role model that was a cartoon character; in the third condition, there was a real aggressive role model. In addition, Bandura presented a control condition with no aggressive role model. The children were then allowed to play with a toy called a Bobo doll, and their aggressive actions were counted. The results demonstrated that the cartoon model produced the highest mean number of aggressive acts. Bandura concluded that the viewing of aggression was not cathartic but led to the modelling of the aggressive behaviour, thus supporting the social-psychological explanation of the social learning of aggression.

- One limitation of this explanation is that it is not able to explain all types of aggression. Whilst it can explain 'pro active' aggression and planned behaviour (for example, where someone has developed the self-efficacy and confidence to repeat aggressive behaviour), it is not able to explain 'reactive' aggression where someone is 'hot headed' or has a reflexive response to a situation or stressor. In this circumstance, there are no predetermined behaviours with rational cognitions and decisions. To explain this type of aggression, a better alternative would be the frustration-aggression hypothesis or a collaboration of both explanations.

- Another strength of this explanation is the practical implications it has for reducing or preventing aggression. For example, media can be created to ensure that viewers are exposed to more pro-social information and characters rather than anti-social ones; through media and school enrichment programmes, anti-crime attitudes can be demonstrated to counteract pro-crime attitudes that may contribute to someone imitating and learning aggression.

- Another limitation of this explanation is that there are many anomalies that the theory cannot explain. For example, someone may observe aggression at home or on the television yet may not choose or be motivated to imitate the behaviour. Whilst some people might repeat a cycle of abuse at home, others may not and instead choose to devote their careers to helping others. This is a limitation because the theory would suggest that if people observe aggression, then there is a good likelihood that it will be imitated, reinforced and learned.

Issues and Debates

- One limitation of the social learning theory of aggression is that it can be criticised for being culturally biased and only considering aggressive behaviour from a western perspective, assuming all cultures have the same values and attitudes towards aggression. Christianson (2006) studied the Kung San people of the Kalahari Desert and found aggressive behaviour was very rare in this society. Kung San parents do not use physical punishment, and there is no value placed on aggressive behaviour. So there are no cultural norms for aggression, and children do not display aggressive behaviour. This study shows the case for social learning being complex and questions whether social learning theory in relation to aggression may only be applied to western cultures.

- Another limitation of this explanation is that it only offers a nomothetic approach to explaining human aggression, suggesting that there is a general rule that can predict aggressive behaviour. For example, the theory claims that it is learned directly or indirectly through observation and reinforcement. However, we are complex individuals, and each go through different experiences, in addition to different physiological changes. These individual, unique influences need to be acknowledged and are overlooked by taking a nomothetic approach rather than an idiographic approach to understanding aggression.

Possible Exam Questions

1. Which one of the following refers to the social learning theory of aggression? (1 mark)
    a) Nature
    b) Nurture
    c) Diathesis Stress Model
    d) Pre-natal influences

2. Explain what is meant by the terms 'observation' and 'imitation' in aggression. (2 marks)
Exam Hint: For this question, you should give a brief definition of both observation and imitation. Imagine that each definition is worth one mark each.

3. Distinguish between 'direct' and 'indirect' learning in aggression. (4 marks)

Exam Hint: You should still remain focused on social learning theory and how aggression may be a behaviour that is learned; however, you must explain the difference between direct and indirect (vicarious) learning.

4. Summarise what is meant by the term 'mediational processes' in relation to human aggression. (4 marks)

Exam Hint: To answer this question, you could explain the purpose of the mediational processes and how cognitive learning was included in the theory. For the other marks, you can give one or two examples of mediational processes but remember to keep focused on aggression.

5. Kieran is in trouble at school for kicking his friend in the shin following a disagreement about the rules of a playground game. The headteacher is aware that Kieran has an older sister in school who is often in trouble for aggressive behaviour towards other people. Use your knowledge of social learning theory to explain aggression. Refer to Kieran in your answer. (6 marks)

Exam Hint: This question is assessing your understanding of social learning theory and how you can apply it to Kieran and his aggressive behaviour. You could talk about mediational processes here, but you may choose o just talk about vicarious learning/indirect learning instead.

6. A Tik Tok creator was banned from using the social media platform after recording a video of being aggressive towards her partner. Before the video was removed from Tik Tok, she had two million followers. Tik Tok claimed that whilst they do not condone violence, they also do not want younger people to see this behaviour and learn it from people that they are fans of. Use your knowledge of social learning theory and aggression to explain why Tik Tok are right in assuming that younger fans may imitate the behaviour. (4 marks)

Exam Hint: In this question, consider the importance of models in social learning theory and why they may be influential in teaching other people how to behave. Avoid being too generic in your answer, and make sure you use social learning theory specialist terms.

7. Discuss the social learning theory of aggression as applied to human behaviour. (8 marks)

Exam Hint: Make sure you think about what the command word 'discuss' means so that you are able to satisfy the marking criteria. The question is an extended writing one, but it is only worth eight marks, so you do need to make sure you select the evaluation points that you want to use for discussion by thinking ahead. Don't forget to include some knowledge.

8. Explain one limitation of the social learning theory of aggression. (4 marks)

Exam Hint: Choose your limitation carefully and opt for one that you can discuss in detail. You only need to offer one, so choose wisely.

9. Outline and evaluate the social learning theory of aggression. (16 marks)

Exam Hint: Whilst you must ensure that you offer a detailed and knowledgeable account of the theory, remember that most marks in this question are for effective evaluation. You can also use your knowledge of issues and debates for discussion, but remember to make your discussion specific and unique to aggression and the social learning theory.

THE ETHOLOGICAL EXPLANATION OF AGGRESSION

Specification: The ethological explanation of aggression, including reference to innate releasing mechanisms and fixed action patterns. Evolutionary explanations of human aggression.

WHAT YOU NEED TO KNOW
⇨ Describe the ethological explanation of aggression.
⇨ Explain innate releasing mechanisms and fixed action patterns.
⇨ Evaluate the ethological explanation of aggression.

The Ethological Explanation of Aggression

Ethological explanations of aggression are based on studies of the innate behaviour of animals (including humans) in their natural environment. The focus of an ethological explanation is to try and account for behaviour in terms of its adaptive value to the specific species. Ethologists believe that looking at animal behaviour can help us to understand human behaviour.

Lorenz (1966) was the founder of ethology and proposed that aggression serves as an adaptive function and establishes dominance hierarchies. He also claimed that aggression is an instinct that all species and all individuals have, regardless of learning or experiences. Aggression is often demonstrated in a series of ritualistic behaviours that sometimes result in death, which also suggests that there are adaptive functions of aggression.

Aggression as an Adaptive Function	Ritualistic Aggression
Animals become aggressive to defeat other animals of the same species and claim their territory. This is adaptive because the species are then spread out in different areas, which reduces the danger of starvation and the competition for resources such as food, safety, and mates.	Lorenz observed that animal fights do not always result in damage or death and that most involve ritualistic behaviours such as signalling. Signalling differs in each species, but examples include baring teeth, standing tall, and displaying claws. Animals also use appeasement gestures to express defeat, such as turning away from the aggressor to show vulnerability. These rituals are adaptive since they avoid death, which would ultimately threaten the existence of a species.

The ethological approach also explains that aggression is a 'fixed action pattern' (FMP) because of an '**innate releasing mechanism**' (IRM). This means that there are biological influences (IRM) that are triggered by environmental stimuli such as threats or frustrations, and the result is a specific sequence of behaviours – the fixed action pattern.

Fixed action patterns are behavioural sequences that occur because of innate releasing mechanisms. For example, when a dog sees a cat running away from them, they have an instinctive response to chase the cat. When the cat is still, the innate releasing mechanism is not activated. Lea (1984) claims that fixed action patterns are:

- ⇨ Not likely to change the sequence
- ⇨ Found in all species
- ⇨ A response to specific stimuli
- ⇨ Likely to occur in specific situations only
- ⇨ Innate, rather than learned
- ⇨ 'Ballistic' and unable to be stopped until the triggered behaviour has been executed

Evaluating the Ethological Explanation of Aggression

- ⇨ One strength of the ethological explanation of aggression is that it is supported by research. Tinbergen (1951) aimed to investigate the demonstration of fixed action patterns in male stickleback fish, which are known to be territorial during mating season in the presence of other male sticklebacks, and all display a red underbelly during this season. The red belly is the stimulus that triggers the IRM and leads to the FAP. When Tinbergen presented sticklebacks with wooden models of different shapes, they would behave aggressively if the model had a red underbelly, regardless of whether the shape resembled a stickleback or not. They did not become aggressive if there was an absence of the red underbelly, even when they were shaped like a stickleback. This shows that there are innate releasing mechanisms in species that lead to aggressive behaviours (FAP).

- One limitation of the explanation is that there is evidence to suggest that aggression is not always ritualistic in animals, as proposed by the ethological theory. Goodall (2010) studied chimpanzee behaviour for over fifty years and observed groups of chimpanzees that waged a brutal war against neighbouring groups of chimpanzees, slaughtering all members of the group. Goodall (2010) referred to this type of gang behaviour as the 'systematic slaughtering' of one group by another stronger group and continued despite appeasement gestures and signals of submission from the chimpanzees in danger. This aggression is hard to explain from an ethological standpoint as the risk of injury to the attacking group is high and thus does not appear to be an adaptive behaviour.

- There are cultural differences in aggression which pose a weakness for the ethological explanation. If all aggression is the result of innate releasing mechanisms, then aggression should be universal rather than culture-dependent. Nisbett (1993) found that there was a higher prevalence of killings amongst white men in the south of America, rather than the north, in response to arguments and provocations. Nisbett concluded that the difference was caused by culture, and aggression was a learned behaviour. This contrasts with the ethological explanation claims that aggression is an evolved and innate, adaptive behaviour.

- Another limitation of the explanation is that some claim that not all fixed action patterns are indeed fixed. There is some evidence that learning and environmental factors can create variation within a species. Therefore, it may be more appropriate to discuss modal action patterns rather than fixed action patterns. Modal action patterns are behaviours that are instinctual such as the desire to chase in dogs (the prey drive), but that differ from one individual within the species compared to others. For example, some dogs may chase cats, but some dogs do not. The differences in behaviour may be down to training or maybe down to species differentiation because of selective breeding of characteristics. This shows that aggression may not be entirely innate or the result of evolution.

Issues and Debates

- One limitation of the ethological explanation is that research in this field attempts to generalise results and conclusions from animals to humans, which impacts the scientific credibility of the theory. This is a limitation because human aggression varies with the use of weapons and levels of violence, and there are psychological stressors that affect humans more than animals, such as financial pressures. This means that the causes of human aggression may not be the same for humans and animals and that the ethological explanation jeopardises its scientific credibility by making generalisations about humans. However, there are studies that show that human aggression may be caused by activity in the limbic system as a response to threats or stimuli, which suggests that just like animals, humans do have innate releasing mechanisms which may lead to aggressive behaviours.

- The ethological explanation can be criticised for being biologically reductionist, assuming that all aggression can be explained through innate drives and responses that are triggered by the environment. It also assumes that we are all influenced by these biological drives and instincts. This is a limitation because it reduces a complex behaviour that has both physical and psychological elements down to one level of explanation rather than adopting a holistic view of aggression and acknowledging the role of various factors such as learning and cognition.

Possible Exam Questions

1. Which one of the following refers to the ethological theory of aggression? (1 mark)
    a) Ritualistic
    b) Fatalistic
    c) Pessimistic
    d) Optimistic

2. Explain what is meant by the term 'innate releasing mechanism.' (2 marks)
Exam Hint: For this question, you need some elaboration; you must keep focused on aggression.

3. Explain what is meant by the term 'fixed action pattern.' (2 marks)
Exam Hint: Avoid the temptation to talk about innate releasing mechanisms here. FAPs do follow the mechanism, but the question requires you to focus on FAPs soley.

4. Summarise what is meant by 'ritualistic' aggression in animals. (4 marks)
Exam Hint: The question is only asking you for knowledge of ritualistic aggression. You also need to ensure you offer sufficient detail and elaboration to earn the four marks available. You could split your answer into the ritualistic behaviours of aggressors and ritualistic behaviours of prey to provide sufficient detail.

5. Molly has a cat, and she notices that when they are in a garden, the next-door neighbour's cat sometimes comes onto the grass. The two cats sit and stare at each other intensely, without breaking eye contact. Molly has noticed that her own cat starts to make hissing noises and only stops when the neighbour's cat turns away. Using your knowledge of the ethological explanation of aggression, explain the behaviour shown by both cats. (6 marks)
Exam Hint: This question assesses your knowledge and application skills. Make sure your answer addresses the behaviours shown by both of the cats, and make links back to ethology.

6. Sammy is walking his dog on the beach like he does most nights. Usually, the dog is well behaved and walks by Sammy's side when off or on the lead. One night whilst walking, the dog spots a rabbit in the sand dunes and starts to run after it. Although Sammy shouts for the dog to stop and to stay, the dog does not listen and keeps running after the rabbit. Referring to the stem, explain the features of fixed action patterns in aggression. (4 marks)
Exam Hint: In this question, there are a lot of things to do. You must refer to the stem to show your application skills, and you must talk about the features of FAP rather than just state what they are. This question is worth four marks, which means elaboration is necessary, but you should carefully plan your answer and be sure to select what you include rather than use everything you know.

7. Outline one strength of the ethological explanation of aggression. (4 marks)
Exam Hint: For four marks, you will need to carefully select a strength that you can explain with detail and elaboration. If you opt to use research support, make sure you focus on why the research is a strength for the explanation.

8. Outline one limitation of the ethological explanation of aggression. (4 marks)
Exam Hint: Choose your limitation carefully and opt for one that you can discuss in detail. You only need to offer one, so choose wisely. Although you may usually counter a limitation with a strength, remain focused on the limitation here.

9. Discuss the ethological explanation of aggression. (16 marks)
Exam Hint: Whilst you must ensure that you offer a detailed and knowledgeable account of the theory, remember that most marks in this question are for effective evaluation. Choose research to support and challenge the theory, but be sure to stay focused on the explanation.

THE EVOLUTIONARY EXPLANATION OF AGGRESSION

Specification: The ethological explanation of aggression, including reference to innate releasing mechanisms and fixed action patterns. Evolutionary explanations of human aggression.

WHAT YOU NEED TO KNOW
➡ Describe the evolutionary explanations of aggression, such as jealousy and bullying.
➡ Explain why aggression is adaptive according to evolutionary explanations.
➡ Evaluate evolutionary explanations of aggression.

The Evolutionary Explanations of Aggression

Buss and Duntley (2006) claim that aggression is an evolved behaviour that serves multiple functions such as mate selection, competing for resources, defeating sexual rivals, increasing status, and dominating hierarchies. Aggression is therefore considered to be an adaptive behaviour that is beneficial for different reasons.

One of the main assumptions is that sexual jealousy is a motivator for aggression and is also an adaptive trait that may have evolved over time as a way to ensure male genes are passed onto their offspring. One **evolutionary** reason why men may experience sexual jealousy is that they can never be as certain as women that their offspring is genetically theirs; instead, they must trust that the female has been faithful and honest about who has fathered their child. This paternal uncertainty stems from cuckolding fears, where men may fear investing their resources, time and emotion into a child that is not genetically theirs whilst being unaware of this. Sexual jealousy may have evolved as an adaptive way to ensure that cuckoldry does not happen, to prevent their partner from cheating or being tempted by other men. Sexual jealousy is stronger in men than women, further demonstrating its evolutionary nature.

In addition to strategies to prevent cuckoldry, the evolutionary explanation of aggression claims that mate retention strategies are also an adaptive response that is likely to lead to aggression. Wilson (1995) found that women who reported their partner using mate retention strategies were also more likely to have experienced domestic violence at the hands of their partners.

Mate retention strategies can include the following behaviours:

➡ **Direct guarding:** males being vigilant about their partner's behaviours, routines or social interactions. For example, checking phones, following their partner or tracking who they speak to.

➡ **Negative inducements:** making threats about the consequences of the female partner leaving or breaking up the relationship, such as threatening to harm themselves or others.

The evolutionary explanation claim that aggression is a naturally selected behaviour, part of our genetics passed down from ancestors because it is a behaviour that leads to benefits. Bullying behaviour is considered to be an adaptive behaviour that increases success with mates, which increases the likelihood of passing genetics onto offspring and reproducing. Bullying behaviour also demonstrates traits such as dominance, fearlessness, strength and resource acquisition, all of which may be attractive to the opposite sex and threatening to rivals. Males demonstrating these traits are more likely to be successful in reproducing, suggesting that bullying behaviours are evolutionary in nature.

Evaluating the Evolutionary Explanations of Aggression

➡ One strength of evolutionary explanations of aggression is that there is research to support the link between mate retention strategies and aggression. Shackelford et al. (2005) studied intimate partner violence in 107 heterosexual, married couples who had been married less than a year. The males completed a survey about their mate retention behaviours, whilst the females completed a survey about the extent of violence their partner demonstrated towards them. There was a strong and positive correlation between the results of the male and the female surveys, suggesting that the more the male partner engaged in mate retention strategies, the more likely they were to exhibit aggressive behaviours. This supports the evolutionary basis of aggression and sexual jealousy as an adaptive behaviour.

- Another strength of evolutionary explanations is that they could lead to real-life applications, such as reducing bullying behaviours and aggression. Volk et al. (2012) state that anti-bullying campaigns that appeal to bullies to stop do not work since they require the bully to give up all the benefits of bullying, such as attracting mates and resources. Based on the evolutionary explanation, the focus of anti-bullying interventions should be on finding more suitable ways for people to demonstrate their power or athleticism, such as in sports or other competitions. This would provide a safe way for people to demonstrate these adaptive traits whilst reducing aggression.

- One limitation of the evolutionary explanation is that it is hard to falsify concepts such as natural selection and adaptive behaviours. In addition, a lot of research is reliant on correlations and, therefore, can only establish a relationship between two variables, such as aggression and mate retention strategies. At best, the explanation is only able to suggest that aggression may be influenced by evolution and ancestor genetics, and the explanation is not compatible with the aims of science, which require a theory to be testable and falsifiable.

- A final strength of evolutionary explanations is that they can account for gender differences in aggression. There are different types of aggression exhibited by men and women, with women more likely to engage in verbal aggression and men more likely to engage in physical aggression. This is adaptive because by avoiding physical aggression, women can ensure their safety and survival, as well as their child's. By using non-aggressive methods of solving disputes and mostly using verbal aggression in conflict situations, women show clear gender differences in aggression. This means that the evolutionary explanation of aggression is able to explain such a difference, whereas other explanations cannot.

Issues and Debates

- One limitation of the explanation is that there is an assumption that aggression is universal and innate, which ignores the role of culture and differences in aggression. The Mundugamoor Tribe in Papa New Guinea is more aggressive than the Arapesh tribe, showing that aggression can differ intra-culturally as well as inter-culturally. In addition, the I Kun San people of the Kalahari are anti-aggression, and anyone exhibiting aggression will find that their status and relationships are jeopardised. This shows that culture does impact aggression and should not be overlooked by the evolutionary explanations.

- Another limitation of the explanation is that it could be regarded as socially sensitive. This is because the explanation attempts to offer scientific explanations for why men behave more aggressively than women and why men may commit domestic violence towards their partners. The explanation suggests that these behaviours are adaptive and inherited from ancestors, rather than free will and choice, which incidentally suggests that men are not responsible for their behaviours. This is not compatible with the justice system or rehabilitation programmes where previously abusive males would be expected to hold themselves accountable for their actions and change.

Possible Exam Questions

1. Which one of the following refers to the evolutionary theory of aggression? (1 mark)
    a) Modelling
    b) Serotonin
    c) Adaptive
    d) Operant

2. Explain what is meant by the term 'natural selection' in aggression. (2 marks)
Exam Hint: For this question, you need some elaboration; you must keep focused on aggression.

3. Explain the relationship between mate retention strategies and aggression. (4 marks)
Exam Hint: You could use research to answer this question, but you must be able to show that you know what mate retention strategies are and how they could lead to aggression – avoid the common mistake of just describing mate retention strategies.

4. Summarise why bullying may be an adaptive behaviour. (4 marks)
Exam Hint: The question is only asking you for your knowledge; however, you need to ensure that you offer sufficient detail and elaboration to earn the four marks available. Try and avoid just listing the potential advantages of bullying – you need to link it to the theory.

5. Kaitlyn has recently moved to a new high school and is being bullied by a group of older girls. The headteacher wants to promote an anti-bullying day, where the consequences of bullying are discussed, along with talks about why bullying must stop. Kaitlyn is worried that this will not help and that the bullies will not be motivated enough to stop. Using your knowledge of evolutionary explanations, suggest why the headteacher's intervention may not be effective and suggest an alternative. (6 marks)
Exam Hint: There is a lot to do in this question. Think about the adaptive benefits of bullying and why being told to stop might not be productive. Don't forget to suggest an alternative – you could think about the positive implications to come from this theory.

6. Tameka is unhappy in her new relationship. Her boyfriend demands to see her phone every night to check her messages, and he gets very angry if she doesn't ring him every hour to tell him where she is and who she is with. He tells her that he loves her and just wants to have a happy relationship, but he has been physically aggressive towards her on several occasions. Use your knowledge of the evolutionary theory to explain the boyfriend's behaviour. (4 marks)
Exam Hint: In this question, you need to show that you understand the theory and that you can make links to the hints in the stem. Look out for the clues about jealousy, and make sure that you make links to aggression, not just jealousy.

7. Outline one strength of the evolutionary explanation of aggression. (4 marks)
Exam Hint: For four marks, you will need to carefully select a strength that you can explain with detail and elaboration. If you opt to use research support, make sure you focus on why the research is a strength for the explanation.

8. Outline one limitation of the evolutionary explanation of aggression. (4 marks)
Exam Hint: Choose your limitation carefully and opt for one that you can discuss in detail. You only need to offer one, so choose wisely. Although you may usually counter a limitation with a strength, remain focused on the limitation here.

9. Outline and evaluate the evolutionary explanation of aggression. (16 marks)
Exam Hint: Make sure you think about what the command word 'discuss' means so that you are able to satisfy the marking criteria. The question is an extended writing one, but it is only worth eight marks, so you do need to make sure you select the evaluation points that you want to use for discussion by thinking ahead. Don't forget to include some knowledge.

INSTITUTIONAL AGGRESSION

Specification: Institutional aggression in the context of prisons: dispositional and situational explanations.

WHAT YOU NEED TO KNOW
➡ Explain reasons for institutional aggression in prison, including dispositional and situational factors.
➡ Evaluate the strengths and limitations of research into institutional aggression.
➡ Assess the implications for the economy deriving from research into institutional aggression.

Explaining Institutional Aggression

Institutional aggression refers to aggressive behaviour that takes place within the confines of an organised setting, such as a **prison**. There are many incidents of aggression and riots inside prisons, and institutional explanations aim to determine why these occur, with the intention of reducing them.

Dispositional explanations refer to any explanation that assumes that aggression is caused by the individual and their personality rather than a consequence of situational factors inside a prison. One dispositional explanation that has been investigated is 'the importation model', proposed by Irwin and Cressey (1962).

The importation model assumes that when an individual commits a crime and receives a custodial sentence, they enter prison with specific traits and learned behaviours. For example, inmates may have a pro-crime attitude and a variety of criminal experiences. In addition to this, inmates also have personal characteristics such as race, gender, class, or religious beliefs. Irwin and Cressey (1962) propose that it is these attitudes and traits that make some inmates likely to continue with criminal behaviours and violence once they are inside prison. In other words, the offenders import these antisocial behaviours into prison and use them to navigate their way through their sentence and to deal with conflicts that may arise with other prisoners.

Situational explanations refer to any explanation that assumes aggression and violence in prison are caused by features of the environment itself rather than the people who are in there. Clemmer (1958) claims that prisoners experiences 'pains of deprivation' inside prison, such as:

➡ Deprivation of freedom and autonomy whilst inside prison
➡ Deprivation of material goods such as money, personal belongings and resources
➡ Deprivation of safety such as fearing for their physical and psychological safety in prison
➡ Deprivation of heterosexual intimacy

This 'deprivation model' assumes that inmates become aggressive as a way of surviving in prison or venting frustration. For example, whilst deprived of material goods, there is competition for resources among all inmates, which could lead to aggression and conflicts. In addition, the inmates may experience frustration if they are bored are deprived of stimulation. Aggression is therefore considered to be the result of pressures and frustrations within the prison situation itself.

Evaluating Institutional Aggression

➡ One strength of the dispositional explanation of institutional aggression is that it is supported by research. DeLisi (2011) investigated the behaviours of juvenile delinquents who entered institutions in California. The inmates shared dispositional traits such as experiences of trauma, aggression, abuse, and addictions. In comparison to a control group, these inmates engaged in more violent behaviours and misconduct inside prison. This shows that dispositional traits do increase the likelihood of inmates becoming aggressive once inside prison, supporting the importation model.

➡ One limitation of research into institutional aggression is that research is inconclusive about what causes aggression. Whilst DeLisi (2011) supports the link between inmate characteristics and aggression, Steiner (2009) found that there were other predictors of aggression in prison. He found that inmate aggression was higher in institutions where they experienced more deprivation and where there was significantly more use of protective custody for safety. This shows that situational factors could be a precursor to violence in prisons, not inmate disposition.

➡ Another limitation of explanations of institutional aggression is that most do not acknowledge the influence of the staff who run prisons. The ACM (administration control model) suggests that aggression in prisons is likely to occur when prisons are not running efficiently; when staff are abusive or distant from inmates; or when there is a lack of opportunity to be rehabilitated. This means that neither the dispositional nor situational explanations of institutional aggression are thorough enough to explain all incidents of violence in prisons.

➡ A final limitation of the research is that not all positive implications have had the desired effect. Hensley et al. (2002) studied male and female inmates who were allowed conjugal visits, which would reduce the deprivation of intimacy. However, incidents of aggression did not reduce as expected, suggesting that situational factors may not be as influential in prison violence as first proposed.

Issues and Debates

➡ One limitation of the institutional explanations of aggression is that they are both reductionist. Both the dispositional and situational explanations assume that violence in prison can be explained with just one influence, either the traits of inmates or the prison itself. Many propose that a more holistic and accurate view of prison aggression is an interactionist model. This model assumes that some inmates enter prison with predispositions for aggression, whilst some do not but become aggressive due to the deprivations in prison. In addition, the model proposes that whilst the importation model can explain inmate on inmate violence, it is the situational explanation that is better suited to explaining why some inmates may be violent towards staff. This suggests that no one single explanation of institutional aggression can explain the broad spectrum of aggressive incidents and that a combined view of explanations is more suitable.

➡ Another limitation of both institutional explanations of aggression is that they could be perceived as socially sensitive. The dispositional explanation assumes that the inmates are predisposed to aggression, which indicates that some rehabilitation methods may not have any impact on reducing aggression or criminal behaviour. The situational explanation assumes that the inmates are suffering in prison and using aggression as a survival behaviour or emotional release. This indicates that the aggression in prisons is not solely the fault of the individual and that it is the prison system itself which needs to change, not the inmate.

Possible Exam Questions

1. Which one of the following refers to 'institutional aggression?' (1 mark)
   a) Aggressive behaviour in an organised setting
   b) Aggressive behaviour in an aggressive setting
   c) Aggressive behaviour in an indoor setting
   d) Aggressive behaviour in an outdoor setting

2. Explain what is meant by 'dispositional explanation' in aggression. (2 marks)
Exam Hint: For this question, you need some elaboration; you must keep focused on aggression.

3. Explain what is meant by 'situational explanation' in aggression. (4 marks)
Exam Hint: You need to give more elaboration here than you would for question two. You can achieve this by talking about the deprivations in prison but avoid merely listing them. You should make links to aggression throughout your answer.

4. Summarise what research has shown about institutional aggression. (4 marks)
Exam Hint: The question is only asking you for your knowledge. There is no set number of studies that you should refer to, but there are four marks to earn, so you should do either one in sufficient detail or more than one in less detail. The key part of this question is the word 'shown', so be sure to focus on the results.

5. Aamir runs a local prison and has seen an increase in the number of inmate-on-inmate violent attacks in the last month. During this month, there has also been an influx of new staff starting and a ban on all social visits due to construction work

taking place. Use your knowledge of institutional aggression to explain why there may be an increase in violence in this prison. (6 marks)
Exam Hint: This question requires you to demonstrate your knowledge and understanding of aggression in prisons and your application skills. Do this by reading the stem carefully and making links between the prompts and the theories.

6. Erin has received a custodial sentence for theft. She has been in prison for a week and is struggling to adapt. She is not allowed out of her cell except for 20 minutes a day when she is expected to get fresh air, exercise, and make any calls. Erin fears being attacked by other inmates and is stir-crazy with boredom. Her sister is worried about how Erin will cope in prison and was surprised to hear that Erin had been in a fight with the person she shares a cell with. Explain the situational explanation of institutional aggression. Refer to Erin in your answer. (4 marks)
Exam Hint: In this question, you need to show that you understand the theory and that you can make links to the hints in the stem. Make sure you focus on the correct explanation and read the stem carefully to pull out relevant links.

7. Outline one strength of dispositional explanations of aggression. (4 marks)
Exam Hint: For four marks, you will need to carefully select a strength that you can explain with detail and elaboration. If you opt to use research support, make sure you focus on why the research is a strength for the explanation. Avoid the temptation to just talk about the study in detail. Your answer should focus on how the study supports the explanation.

8. Outline one limitation of situational explanations of aggression. (4 marks)
Exam Hint: Choose your limitation carefully and opt for one that you can discuss in detail. You don't have to offer countercriticisms here, but you do need to elaborate sufficiently to earn the four marks.

9. Discuss institutional explanations of aggression. (16 marks)
Exam Hint: Make sure you think about what the command word 'discuss' means so that you are able to satisfy the marking criteria. The question is an extended writing one, but it is only worth eight marks, so you do need to make sure you select the evaluation points that you want to use for discussion by thinking ahead. Don't forget to include some knowledge.

MEDIA INFLUENCES ON AGGRESSION

Specification: Media influences on aggression, including the effects of computer games. The role of desensitisation, disinhibition, and cognitive priming.

WHAT YOU NEED TO KNOW
⇨ Describe research that investigates the effects of computer games on aggression.
⇨ Discuss the role of desensitisation, disinhibition, and cognitive priming in aggression.
⇨ Assess the impact of media such as video games on aggression.

Media is something that most people are exposed to or engage in, such as television, gaming, music, films, or education. Researchers are interested in the effect media has on our behaviour and whether it causes aggression or whether people are drawn to certain genres of media because of a predisposition. For example, will someone become aggressive if they play aggressive computer games, or do they play aggressive computer games because their disposition draws them to the games?

Researching the Effects of Computer Games on Aggression

Video games are played by many young people and adults, and there are genres of games such as simulations, sports, shooting and many more. There is much debate about the relationship between playing computer games and levels of aggression, and there is a wealth of research in this area. For example, social learning theories claim that people will learn aggressive behaviour if they observe aggression in media and games, whilst operant conditioning theories may claim that aggressive behaviours are learned through positive reinforcement.

There have been plenty of different research methods used to investigate the effect of computer games on aggression. For example:

Researcher/s	Methodology	Results	Conclusion
Bartholow and Anderson (2002)	A lab experiment was conducted to see playing aggressive computer games led to aggression. Participants either played an aggressive game (Mortal Kombat) or a non-aggressive game (Golf) for ten minutes. They were then asked to give blasts of white noise to an 'opponent', a standard measure of aggression in research.	Those who played the aggressive game delivered a mean of 5.9 decibels of white noise, whilst those who played the non-aggressive game delivered a mean of 4.6 decibels.	Playing an aggressive video game increases the likelihood that people will behave aggressively towards others.
DeLisi et al. (2013)	A correlational study was conducted using structured interviews with juvenile offenders and reviewing their previous aggressive behaviours. The interviews asked them about their game playing and assessed aggression.	The delinquents had histories of violence and/or gang behaviour. These aggressive behaviours correlated with the aggression measures and reports of gaming in the interviews.	There is a positive correlation between computer gaming and aggression. The more someone engages in aggressive computer games, the more aggressive they will behave.

Evaluating the Effects of Computer Games on Aggression

- One limitation of relying on correlational research to investigate the relationship between aggression and computer games is that they only offer a bidirectional conclusion. Whilst research suggests that playing aggressive computer games leads to aggressive behaviours, it is also just as likely that aggressive people will be drawn to playing aggressive video games. This means that correlational research is not able to establish a cause and effect conclusion about aggression, which will then impact the usefulness of the research.

- Another limitation of experiments that investigate aggression and computer gaming is that they often split participants up into different conditions to play 'distinctive' games. For example, some participants will play an aggressive game, and some will play non-aggressive games. However, there is no way to ensure that the games are as distinct as researchers believe. Some games involve adaptive play where the game can be played aggressively or prosocially, depending on the choices made by the player. In addition, some sports games are considered non-aggressive but still have elements of competitiveness and frustration. This means that research that compares the effects of different computer games could lack validity if the games are not truly distinctive.

- One strength comes from the range of research to support the effect of computer games on aggression. Anderson et al. (2010) conducted a meta-analysis, reviewing 136 studies. Results suggested that exposure to violent computer games was associated with increases in aggressive thoughts, feelings and behaviours, regardless of cultural differences. This supports other research that concludes that exposure to aggressive computer gaming is implicated in the development of aggressive behaviours.

- A final limitation of research in this field is that most experiments lack ecological validity in the way they measure aggression. Researchers must investigate and measure aggressive behaviours ethically; however, this impacts the realism of the study. For example, measuring aggression with the decibels of white noise played to opponents ensures that participants are protected from harm, but it is an unrealistic example of aggression. Since aggression in experiments must be operationalised in such ways, it means that research conclusions may not be as helpful in reducing aggression in real life as first intended.

Explaining the Role of Desensitisation, Disinhibition, And Cognitive Priming

DeWall and Anderson (2011) propose a general aggression model to explain aggression, which states that aggression is such a broad behaviour and is different in everyone who displays it that no one explanation alone is sufficient. Instead, it is likely that individuals who behave aggressively because of media exposure are influenced by **desensitisation, disinhibition,** and **cognitive priming**, not just one isolated influence.

Desensitisation refers to the reduction in arousal or anxiety in response to aggression in media because of being exposed to it too frequently. Normally, aggressive media evokes a physiological reaction in individuals through the nervous system; however, when children and adults are repeatedly exposed to it, this diminishes over time, and they become desensitised to its effect. Another effect of repeated exposure to aggressive media is psychological changes, such as learning a pro-crime attitude and a decrease in empathy when people are hurt or victims of aggression.

Disinhibition refers to the reduction of social and psychological inhibitions about aggressive behaviour. Most people are aware that such behaviours are antisocial and unacceptable; however, with repeated exposure to media that may positively reinforce aggressive behaviour, some people become disinhibited. Aggressive media normalises what should remain deviant, and this can lead to new or changed social norms in people, groups, or societies.

Cognitive priming refers to 'script' learning, meaning that when we are exposed to aggressive media, they can often provide a framework for how aggressive situations usually occur. This is stored in memory, making us 'primed' to be aggressive or engage in antisocial behaviour when we feel the situation warrants it.

Evaluating the Role of Desensitisation, Disinhibition, And Cognitive Priming

- One strength of these explanations is that they are supported by research. For example, Weisz and Earls (1995) conducted a study to investigate the effect of watching violent media on aggression. Some participants watched the film 'Straw Dogs', which includes graphic scenes of sexual violence. They then watched a re-enacted rape trial, and their attitudes and behaviours were compared to a control group who had watched a non-violent film instead. The male participants who watched Straw Dogs showed more acceptance of aggression and were less sympathetic towards the victim and found the defendant guilty. This shows that exposure to aggressive media led to desensitisation.

- Further research support comes from Berkowitz and Alioto (1973), who found that when participants watched media containing aggression as vengeance, they were more likely to administer shocks (fake) more frequently and longer-lasting to a confederate. From this, Berkowitz and Alioto (1973) claim that when aggression is seen as justified, people are disinhibited and are more likely to consider aggressive behaviour as socially acceptable.

- One strength of cognitive priming explanations of aggression is that they could lead to implications for reducing aggression. If people become aggressive because they learn 'scripts' from media, and are exposed to so much aggressive media that they become ready to perceive the world as threatening, then this means that media could be used to counter this effect. For example, media could be a medium for showcasing alternative behaviours to aggression, conflict resolution or even to ensure that antisocial media is outweighed by anti-crime attitudes.

- One limitation of these explanations of aggression and media is that there are other alternative theories. Psychodynamic explanations suggest that people watch aggressive media because it is cathartic, allowing people to release tensions or fulfil aggressive behaviours vicariously. However, this explanation does not have as much empirical evidence for it since concepts such as catharsis are not as testable as disinhibition or desensitisation.

Issues and Debates

- One limitation of these explanations of aggression is that they can be criticised for being environmentally reductionist. They assume that all aggression occurs because of exposure to media, regardless of culture or type of aggression. This assumes that there are no other significant influences on behaviour that could lead to aggression when there are actually several credible explanations that are perhaps supported by more objective evidence, such as biological theories.

- One limitation of these explanations is that they could be considered socially sensitive. Whether the research focuses on the effects of computer gaming or cognitive priming, the explanations assume that individuals become aggressive due to external influences. Whilst this provides good opportunities to change media and reduce aggression, they avoid holding individuals to account for their own decisions and behaviours, which is not compatible with the justice system.

Possible Exam Questions

1. Which one of the following refers to why some become aggressive? (1 mark)
   a) Cognitive priming
   b) Cognitive error
   c) Cognitive dysfunction
   d) Cognitive learning

2. Explain what is meant by the term 'disinhibition' in aggression. (2 marks)
Exam Hint: For this question, you need some elaboration; you must keep focused on aggression.

3. Summarise what research suggests about the effects of computer games on aggression. (4 marks)
Exam Hint: Focus on the word 'suggests' here, rather than merely describing research into this area. The question requires you to talk about findings/conclusions, so this should be your focus. You may choose to refer to one piece of research in detail but may find it easier to reach full marks by doing more than one in less detail.

4. Summarise how some people may become desensitised to aggression. (3 marks)
Exam Hint: This question requires you to do more than define what desensitisation means. You need to offer sufficient elaboration but avoid becoming anecdotal in your answer.

5. Sofia and April have both got a PlayStation for Christmas. Sofia enjoys playing games such as Grand Theft Auto and wrestling games, whilst April prefers farm simulation games. They are both reaching their targets in school, and April has received a certificate for helpful behaviour towards others. However, Sofia's teacher has asked to speak to her parents about her

aggressive behaviour towards staff. Use your knowledge of media and aggression to explain the difference between Sofia and April. (6 marks)

Exam Hint: Although the question focuses on media and aggression, you should read the stem carefully and notice that the focus is on computer games. Make sure you refer to both Sofia and April and make a clear distinction between their behaviours.

6. Garth is completing research on the effects of aggressive films on behaviour. He asked participants who watch at least one aggressive film a week to complete a survey that measures aggressive thoughts and responses to hypothetical scenarios. He also asked participants who didn't watch aggressive films at all to complete the same survey. The participants who watched the aggressive films scored higher for aggressive responses and thoughts than those who did not watch the films. Using your knowledge of media and aggression, explain why the conclusions drawn from this study may lack validity. (4 marks)

Exam Hint: Although this is a media and aggression question, you are also being tested on your application of research methodology knowledge. Consider the way aggression has been measured, and consider the controls that may be needed in research where participants are watching films. Think ahead about your answer – this will need structure.

7. Outline one strength of research into media and aggression. (4 marks)

Exam Hint: For four marks, you will need to carefully select a strength that you can explain with detail and elaboration. If you opt to use research support, make sure you focus on why the research is a strength for the explanation. Alternatively, you could consider the implications that could come from the research.

8. Discuss media influences on aggression. (16 marks)
9. Discuss research into the effects of computer gaming on aggression. (16 marks)

Exam Hint: Make sure you think about what the command word 'discuss' means so that you are able to satisfy the marking criteria. The question is an extended writing one, but it is only worth eight marks, so you do need to make sure you select the evaluation points that you want to use for discussion by thinking ahead. Don't forget to include some knowledge.

Discuss the role of genetic factors in aggression. (16 marks)

The biological approach assumes that aggression is caused by genetics and that it is very much a hereditary behaviour. One proposal is that abnormal chromosomes at conception cause aggression later in life, such as the XYY chromosome pattern. Furthermore, researchers have investigated the link between genetics and aggression through a variety of methods, such as twin studies, family studies and adoption studies. Geneticists have investigated aggression amongst twins, expecting that there would be higher concordance amongst monozygotic twins (identical) than dizygotic twins (non-identical). Since monozygotic twins are 100% genetically identical in contrast to non-identical twins, the higher concordance rates would support the role of genes in aggression.

Another assumption is that a faulty MAOA gene is responsible for aggression. Usually, the MAOA gene helps to regulate levels and production of the chemical 'MAOA', which is crucial for avoiding excessive neurochemical availability in the synapse. However, when there is a fault with this gene, levels of MAOA are inhibited, which creates problems for neuron systems in the brain. This would lead to an imbalance of chemicals such as serotonin and dopamine, which would then cause aggression. For example, high levels of dopamine are linked to aggression, and low levels of serotonin (which usually helps us to feel calm) are also linked to aggression.

One strength of the genetic explanation of aggression is that there is a wealth of research evidence in support of the theory. Godar et al. (2014) used selective breeding to remove the MAOA gene in mice, to see what effect this would have on their behaviour. The mice became more aggressive, and they had disrupted levels of serotonin. They also found that when the mice were given medication to help balance their serotonin levels, the aggressive behaviour stopped. This supports the role of genetics in aggression and the influence that genetics can have on neurotransmitters. However, there are extrapolation issues with research on animals that affect how well results and conclusions can be generalised to humans. For example, the aggression that humans demonstrate is both psychological and physical, and since this distinction cannot be made in an animal sample, the results lack the validity needed to help us learn about why humans become aggressive and what we can do to reduce aggression.

One strength regarding the link between the MAOA gene and aggression is that other research has found that an increase in MAOA leads to increased prosocial behaviour and cooperation. In addition to this, the role of genetics in aggression is also supported by research by Brunner (1993). Brunner undertook a study on the males in a large family from the Netherlands, whose members were displaying high levels of aggression. Examples included attempted rape, arson, and impulsive aggression. Five of the males were found to have the dysfunctional version of the MAOA gene, which suggests that this genetic fault is the cause of their aggression.

One limitation of the genetic explanation is that it is criticised for being biologically reductionist. This means that it reduces a complex trait like aggression down to the lowest level of explanation, choosing to focus on genetics at the expense of other influences such as neuroanatomy, stress or relationships. This is a limitation because there are several factors that influence our behaviour, and different people are also likely to be aggressive for different reasons. This means that an explanation of aggression needs to acknowledge how complex the trait is and avoid breaking it down into just one testable cause. However, being biologically reductionist is not always a limitation. The genetic explanation has been able to isolate one gene that could be contributing to aggression, and therefore this can be used to implement interventions to reduce aggression. Without a reductionist approach to investigating aggression, these interventions would not exist.

(~625 Words)
Examiner style comments: *Mark band 4*
This is a well-detailed and accurate essay which provides a solid outline of the role of genetics in aggression. The essay provides a thorough and effective discussion of genetics and aggression. An impressive use of and range of specialist terminology is presented throughout.

Discuss the role of neural and/or hormonal mechanisms in aggression. (16 marks)

Neural mechanisms refer to the brain, whilst hormonal mechanisms refer to the regulation and production of chemicals in the body, and both are implicated in aggression. For example, testosterone is a dominant hormone in men, and males are stereotypically more masculine and aggressive than females, suggesting that testosterone may play a key role in aggression.

Neural mechanisms focus on the limbic system of the brain, which is responsible for regulating our emotional behaviours such as aggression. The limbic system has physical connections to the prefrontal cortex, which is involved in forward planning and reward anticipation, so if there is a problem with the structure of the prefrontal cortex, this could result in reactive aggression. In addition, structural issues in the limbic system affect the way we respond to situations and perceived threats, suggesting that neuroanatomical structure is significant in aggression.

In addition, serotonin is a neurotransmitter that helps us to feel calm, so when the levels of this chemical are too low, this prevents someone from controlling their aggressive behaviour and impulsivity. Those who have abnormal levels of serotonin will therefore struggle to anticipate risk appropriately, leading to risk-taking behaviours, including aggression.

One limitation of this explanation of aggression is that it could be considered gender-biased. Many of the studies used to support it are only conducted on male samples. This is beta bias, as the researchers assume that the findings from male samples can also be used to explain female aggression and behaviours. This is a limitation because it minimises the differences between men and women and fails to acknowledge differences that would matter. For example, women have higher levels of the hormone oxytocin which means they respond to stress and threats in a very different way than males. Just this one hormonal difference alone suggests that men cannot represent women in aggression research.

Another limitation of this explanation is that many argue it is bidirectional. For example, whilst Raine et al. (1997) found that murderers had reduced activity in the prefrontal cortex compared to non-murderers, cause and effect cannot be established. Similarly, if an aggressive person has high levels of testosterone, cause and effect cannot be established here either. This is because whilst the brain and hormones/neurotransmitters may lead to aggression, they may also be affected by the aggression. In other words, it is not possible to know whether the biological abnormalities precede or follow aggression. However, this explanation has led to various interventions for aggression, such as hormone therapy to help reduce aggression. This suggests that this explanation of aggression has been able to contribute to the prevention and reduction of aggression, which may also positively affect crime rates.

There is research to challenge the role of testosterone in aggression. Carre and Mehta (2011) offer a dual hormone hypothesis, claiming that testosterone levels only lead to aggression if cortisol levels are low and that when cortisol levels are high, aggression influenced by testosterone is prevented. Cortisol is a stress hormone and is now implicated in aggression, suggesting that assumptions about testosterone are either inaccurate or misunderstood.

(~500 Words)
Examiner style comments: *Mark band 4*
This is a strong response to this question. The answer provides detailed knowledge of the role of neural and/or hormonal mechanisms in aggression, which is highly accurate. Discussion is thorough and effective, with excellent use of specialist terminology.

Discuss evolutionary explanations of human aggression. (16 marks)

According to evolutionary explanations, aggression is a behaviour that is advantageous for survival and reproduction. One suggestion is that aggression has evolved in males to ensure that they are not 'cuckolded'; in other words, to ensure that they are the true paternal parent of their offspring and are not investing their resources and time into a child that is not genetically theirs. Sexual jealousy may have evolved as an adaptive way to ensure that cuckoldry does not happen, to prevent their partner from cheating or being tempted by other men. Sexual jealousy is stronger in men than women, further demonstrating its evolutionary nature.

Evolutionary explanations also assume that mate retention strategies that involve aggression occur to ensure reproduction. For example, 'direct guarding' (possessive and always knowing your partners' whereabouts) and 'negative inducements' (threats to deter infidelity) are often associated with aggression and reported by women who have experienced domestic violence.

One strength of evolutionary explanations of aggression is that there is research to support the link between mate retention strategies and aggression. Shackelford et al. (2005) studied intimate partner violence in 107 heterosexual, married couples who had been married less than a year. The males completed a survey about their mate retention behaviours, whilst the females completed a survey about the extent of violence their partner demonstrated towards them. There was a strong and positive correlation between the results of the male and the female surveys, suggesting that the more the male partner engaged in mate retention strategies, the more likely they were to exhibit aggressive behaviours. However, there is an assumption that aggression is universal and innate, which ignores the role of culture and differences in aggression. The Mundugamoor tribe in Papa New Guinea are more aggressive than the Arapesh tribe, showing that aggression can differ intra-culturally as well as inter-culturally. This shows that culture does impact aggression and should not be overlooked by the evolutionary explanations.

One limitation of the explanation is that it could be regarded as socially sensitive. This is because the explanation attempts to offer scientific explanations for why men behave more aggressively than women and why men may commit domestic violence towards their partners. The explanation suggests that these behaviours are adaptive and inherited from ancestors, rather than free will and choice, which is not compatible with the justice system or rehabilitation programmes.

One strength of evolutionary explanations is that they can account for gender differences in aggression. There are different types of aggression exhibited by men and women, with women more likely to engage in verbal aggression and men more likely to engage in physical aggression. This is adaptive because by avoiding physical aggression, women can ensure their safety and survival, as well as their child's. By using nonaggressive methods of solving disputes and mostly using verbal aggression in conflict situations, women show a clear gender difference in aggression. This means that the evolutionary explanation of aggression can explain such a difference, whereas other explanations cannot.

(~500 Words)
Examiner style comments: *Mark band 4*
A well-detailed and accurate essay that outlines evolutionary explanations of aggression. The evaluation is thorough and effective. Specialist terminology is used throughout the essay and adds to the quality of the discussion.

Describe and evaluate the social learning theory of human aggression. (16 marks)

According to the social learning theory, aggression is not a biologically driven behaviour. Instead, aggression is a learned behaviour that is acquired through observation of other people and their aggression. The social learning theory assumes that we learn aggression directly, through our own observations and imitations of other people, and from receiving direct reinforcements such as reputations or resources. Alternatively, the social learning theory also assumes that most of our aggression is learned indirectly by seeing the reinforcements and consequences that other people (models) experience. For example, if we see someone rewarded for aggression, then we indirectly observe that aggression leads to positive outcomes, and we may vicariously learn aggression.

The social learning theory also acknowledges that there are cognitions involved in learning behaviours. For example, when we observe other people, we are using the cognitive skill of attention. When we draw on our memories of what aggression we have seen so that we can imitate it, we are using the cognitive skills of retention. Reproduction is required to physically imitate the behaviour and to determine if we are physically capable of doing so, and motivation is a crucial cognitive factor that determines when someone does go onto imitate and reproduce the aggressive behaviour or not.

One strength of the social learning theory of aggression is that it is supported by a wealth of empirical evidence. For example, Bandura (1963) conducted a study with three experimental conditions: in one condition, there was a filmed aggressive role model; in another, there was an aggressive role model that was a cartoon character; in the third condition, there was a real aggressive role model. In addition, Bandura presented a control condition with no aggressive role model. The children were then allowed to play with a toy called a Bobo doll, and their aggressive actions were counted. The results demonstrated that the cartoon model produced the highest mean number of aggressive acts. Bandura concluded that the viewing of aggression was not cathartic but led to the modelling of aggressive behaviour, thus supporting the social-psychological explanation of aggression. However, there are many criticisms of this study, including the nature of the bobo doll. Since a bobo doll is intended to be hit, many believe that these children were not behaving aggressively but were playing the way the toy intended them to. This suggests that there are some internal validity issues with the study, which impacts how much support this study can provide for the social learning theory of aggression.

One limitation of the social learning theory of aggression is that it can be criticised for being culturally biased and only considering aggressive behaviour from a western perspective, assuming all cultures have the same values and attitudes towards aggression. Christianson (2006) studied the Kung San people of the Kalahari Desert and found aggressive behaviour was very rare in this society. Kung San parents do not use physical punishment, and there is no value placed on aggressive behaviour. So, there are no cultural norms for aggression, and children do not display aggressive behaviour. This study shows the case for social learning being complex and questions whether social learning theory in relation to aggression may only be applied to western cultures. However, despite this, the social learning theory does have practical implications it has for reducing or preventing aggression. For example, media can be created to ensure that viewers are exposed to more pro-social information and characters rather than anti-social, and through media and school enrichment programmes, anti-crime attitudes can be demonstrated to counteract pro-crime attitudes that may contribute to someone imitating and learning aggression.

(~600 Words)
Examiner style comments: *Mark band 4*
This is a well-detailed and accurate account of the social learning theory of aggression. The evaluation is thorough and effective in most places, and research is used to strengthen the discussion of the social learning theory.

Outline and evaluate one social psychological theory of aggression. (16 marks)

The deindividuation explanation of aggression proposes that aggression occurs when we lose our sense of self-awareness by becoming part of a crowd. Deindividuation is a psychological state that involves a loss of personal identity and responsibility for your actions. Anyone who becomes deindividuated is more likely to behave aggressively and antisocially due to a feeling of being free from social constraints and the judgement of other people. Deindividuation can occur when we are part of a larger crowd, such as at a football match. Usually, we are distinguishable and identifiable, which keeps us aware of our behaviours and morals. However, a crowd can make you feel anonymous and lose your sense of responsibility for the way that you behave since you are less likely to stand out in the crowd, and this reduces any guilt you may have otherwise experienced about your behaviour.

When we are deindividuated, we behave irrationally, impulsively, and we are in a state of disinhibition. We lose our private self-awareness (awareness of our own guilt, behaviour and morals), and we lose our public self-awareness (awareness of what other people may think of us), which means that we are more likely to behave aggressively and in ways that we would not normally entertain.

One limitation of this explanation of aggression is that it could be considered socially sensitive. This is because the assumption that all crowds and all uniforms will lead to aggression is not entirely accurate but could lead to serious implications. Johnson and Downing (1979) found that when participants were asked to give electric shocks to a confederate, they were less likely to give them shocks if they were dressed as a nurse (a prosocial uniform) and more likely to give shocks if they were dressed in a KKK (Klu Klux Klan) uniform. This suggests that aggression is largely dependent on the type of uniform someone wears or the type of crowd that they are in, such as a church choir.

One strength of this explanation is that there is research to support the link between aggression and deindividuation. Dodd (1985) asked 229 undergraduate psychology students: 'if you could do anything humanly possible with complete assurance that you would not be detected or held responsible, what would you do?' Three independent raters rated the students' responses into those that were antisocial or not. The results found that 36% of the responses were antisocial and 26% were criminal (types of responses referring to acts such as 'robbing a bank'). This research demonstrates the connection between deindividuation as a result of anonymity and subsequent aggression.

However, there is conflicting research. Gerges et al. (1973) found that when eight strangers were placed in a dark room together for an hour with no rules to follow and told that they would never see each other again, it did not take long for talking to cease and for kissing each other to start. In another study, they were told that they would see each again, and this time they did not kiss each other. However, aggression was not demonstrated in either study, suggesting that deindividuation does not inevitably lead to aggression. This conflicting research suggests that the link between deindividuation and aggression remains unclear and that perhaps there are more influencing factors that need to be considered, such as biological predispositions, especially since not everyone enters the deindividuated state in a crowd, disguise, or in the dark.

(~575 Words)
Examiner style comments: *Mark band 4*
This essay demonstrates an exceptionally clear understanding and appreciation of the topic. The knowledge is excellent, and the evaluation is thorough and focused. The evaluation draws on suitable issues and debates and research evidence to provide an interesting commentary.

Discuss explanations of institutional aggression. (16 marks)

Institutionalised aggression refers to any aggressive behaviour that takes place in an organised environment where there are rules and regulations in place to control behaviour, for example, in prison. Aggression in an institution such as prison is believed to occur because of dispositional influences and situational influences. Dispositional explanations refer to any explanation that assumes that aggression is caused by the individual and their personality, rather than a consequence of situational factors inside a prison, such as 'the importation model'.

The importation model assumes that when individuals commit a crime and receive a custodial sentence, they enter prison with traits or learned behaviours. For example, inmates may have a pro-crime attitude and a variety of criminal experiences. In addition to this, inmates also have personal characteristics such as race, gender, class, or religious beliefs. Irwin and Cressey (1962) propose that it is these attitudes and traits that make some inmates likely to continue with criminal behaviours and violence once they are inside prison. Alternatively, the situational explanations assume that the environment causes aggression, such as the deprivation that prisoners experiences during their custodial sentence. Clemmers (1958) claims that prisoners turn violent because of the deprivation they experience, such as deprivation of goods and deprivation of heterosexual relationships.

One limitation of the institutional explanations of aggression is that they are both reductionist. Both the dispositional and situational explanations assume that violence in prison can be explained with just one influence, either the traits of an inmate or the prison itself. Many propose that a more holistic and accurate view of prison aggression is an interactionist model. This model assumes that some inmates enter prison with predispositions for aggression, whilst some do not but become aggressive due to the deprivations in prison. However, there is evidence to support the dispositional explanation of institutional aggression. DeLisi (2011) investigated the behaviours of juvenile delinquents who entered institutions in California. The inmates shared dispositional traits such as experiences of trauma, aggression, abuse, and addictions. In comparison to a control group, these inmates engaged in more violent behaviours and misconduct inside prison. This shows that dispositional traits do increase the likelihood of inmates becoming aggressive once inside prison, supporting the importation model.

One limitation of explanations of institutional aggression is that most do not acknowledge the influence of the staff who run the prisons. The ACM (administration control model) suggests that aggression in prisons is likely to occur when prisons are not running efficiently; when staff are abusive or distant from inmates; or where there is a lack of opportunity to be rehabilitated. This means that neither the dispositional nor situational explanations of institutional aggression are thorough enough to explain all incidents of violence in prisons. Although these alternative explanations would provide opportunities to reduce aggression in prison, such as training staff on conflict management and building relationships with prisoners, situational explanations are also able to offer suggestions for improvement. For example, there could be reviews about relaxing the deprivations within prisons, or the structural design of prisons could acknowledge the need for more personal space. However, the importation model, on the other hand, is not able to offer many suggestions on how to reduce aggression, suggesting this may be an inferior explanation of institutional aggression.

(~550 words)
Examiner style comments: *Mark band 4*
This is a highly detailed and accurate essay examining institutional explanations of aggression. The use of specialist terminology is impressive, and the evaluation is focused, thorough and effective.

Discuss media influences on aggression. (16 marks)

Media refers to a variety of communication channels such as television, films and computer games. There is a general assumption that when people are exposed to media containing aggressive and antisocial behaviours, they are more likely to become aggressive themselves. DeWall and Anderson (2011) propose that it is likely that individuals who behave aggressively because of media exposure are influenced by desensitisation, disinhibition, and cognitive priming, not just one isolated influence.

Desensitisation refers to the reduction in arousal or anxiety in response to aggression in media because of being exposed to it too frequently. For example, if someone witnesses a lot of aggression in their computer games or films, then they become desensitised to it and do not physiologically respond to it the way someone else might respond. In addition to this, disinhibition refers to the reduction of social and psychological inhibitions relating to aggressive behaviour. Most people are aware that such behaviours are antisocial and unacceptable; however, with repeated exposure to media that may positively reinforce aggressive behaviour, some people become disinhibited. Finally, cognitive priming occurs when people who are repeatedly exposed to aggressive media begin to use it as a 'script' for how they should behave in real life, meaning that people are 'primed' to become aggressive in certain situations.

One strength of these explanations is that they are supported by research. For example, Weisz and Earls (1995) conducted a study to investigate the effect of watching violent media on aggression. Some participants watched the film Straw Dogs', which includes graphic scenes of sexual violence. They then watched a re-enacted rape trial, and their attitudes and behaviours were compared to a control group who had watched a non-violent film instead. The male participants who watched Straw Dogs showed more acceptance of aggression and were less sympathetic towards the victim and found the defendant guilty. This shows that exposure to aggressive media led to desensitisation. However, there are other alternative theories. Psychodynamic explanations suggest that people watch aggressive media because it is cathartic, allowing people to release tensions or fulfil aggressive behaviours vicariously.

There is a wealth of research to support the role of computer games in aggression. Bartholow and Anderson (2002) conducted a lab experiment to see if playing aggressive computer games led to aggression. Participants either played an aggressive game (Mortal Kombat) or a non-aggressive game (Golf) for ten minutes. They were then asked to give blasts of white noise to an 'opponent', a standard measure of aggression in research. Those who played the aggressive game delivered a mean of 5.9 decibels of white noise, whilst those who played the non-aggressive game delivered a mean of 4.6 decibels. This suggests that playing an aggressive video game increases the likelihood that people will behave aggressively towards others.

One limitation of these explanations is that they could be considered socially sensitive. Whether the research focuses on the effects of computer gaming or cognitive priming, the explanations assume that individuals become aggressive due to external influences. Whilst this provides good opportunities to change media and reduce aggression, they avoid holding individuals to account for their own decisions and behaviours, which is not compatible with the justice system. However, cognitive priming explanations could lead to implications for reducing aggression. If people become aggressive because they learn 'scripts' from media and are exposed to so much aggressive media that they become ready to perceive the world as threatening, then this means that media could be used to counter this effect. For example, media could be a medium for showcasing alternative behaviours to aggression, conflict resolution or even to ensure that antisocial media is outweighed by anti-crime attitudes.

(~600 Words)
Examiner style comments: *Mark band 4*
This is a well-detailed essay which explains media influence on aggression thoroughly. The evaluation is generally effective, and research is used to strengthen the discussion throughout the essay. The use of specialist terminology is consistent throughout.

Outline and evaluate the dispositional explanation for institutional aggression in prisons. (16 marks)

The dispositional explanation for institutional aggression refers to the individual traits and characteristics of prisoners that enter the prison rather than those that develop during the custodial sentence. One dispositional explanation is the 'importation model', which assumes that any aggression that occurs inside a prison is caused by events or circumstances that occurred outside of prison. For example, some people may be aggressive inside prison because they were always aggressive outside of prison, whilst some people may have learned aggression as part of belonging to a gang or a pro-crime family. Other traits that are imported into prisons include age, religion, experiences, and trauma. Irwin and Cressey (1962) propose that it is these attitudes and traits that make some inmates likely to continue with criminal behaviours and violence once they are inside prison. In other words, the offenders import these antisocial behaviours into prison and use them to navigate their way through their sentence and to deal with conflicts that may arise with other prisoners.

One strength of the dispositional explanation of institutional aggression is that it is supported by research. DeLisi (2011) investigated the behaviours of juvenile delinquents who entered institutions in California. The inmates shared dispositional traits such as experiences of trauma, aggression, abuse, and addictions. In comparison to a control group, these inmates engaged in more violent behaviours and misconduct inside prison. This shows that dispositional traits do increase the likelihood of inmates becoming aggressive once inside prison, supporting the importation model. However, research is inconclusive about what causes aggression. Whilst DeLisi (2011) supports the link between inmate characteristics and aggression, Steiner (2009) found that there were other predictors of aggression in prison. He found that inmate aggression was higher in institutions where they experienced more deprivation and where there was significantly more use of protective custody for safety. This shows that situational factors could be a precursor to violence in prisons, not inmate disposition.

One limitation of the dispositional explanation is that it could be criticised for being socially sensitive as it assumes that the inmates are predisposed to aggression, which indicates that some rehabilitation methods may not have any impact on reducing aggression or criminal behaviour. However, it is reductionist to assume that all aggression in institutions is caused by the people in them when a more holistic view would be to acknowledge the role of situational factors, such as the deprivations of prison. Situational explanations propose that deprivations of goods, heterosexual relationships and deprivation of safety are all key influences in aggression in prison; therefore, a more holistic explanation would be that some people have a disposition that makes them likely to be aggressive in prison, but a situational factor would be the trigger, resulting in aggression.

One limitation of the dispositional explanation of institutional aggression is that the opportunities for reducing prison violence are minimal. If aggression is imported into the prison, then there are limited things that can be done to reduce aggression. It may be more beneficial to acknowledge the influence of the staff who run the prisons. The ACM (administration control model) suggests that aggression in prisons is likely to occur when prisons are not running efficiently; when staff are abusive or distant from inmates; or where there is a lack of opportunity to be rehabilitated. This means that neither the dispositional nor situational explanations of institutional aggression are thorough enough to explain all incidents of violence in prisons. The ACM is also able to offer more implications for change and reducing aggression in prisons. For example, staff could be trained in conflict resolution and in communication with inmates, and institutions could invest in educational schemes to support rehabilitation.

(~600 Words)
Examiner style comments: *Mark band 4*
This is a well-structured and clear essay which provides an accurate and well-detailed account of institutional explanations of aggression. The essay is clear, coherent, and focused, and specialist terminology is used throughout. Research is used effectively to build discussion.

> Micah was experiencing outbursts of temper at home and school. His friends and family were concerned that he seemed to have no control over his temper. Micah has two older sisters, and they are both doing very well in school and are calm and easy-going. Micah's grandfather had spent some time in prison for arson, and Micah's father had died when Micah was younger in a fight.

Using your knowledge of the genetic, neural and hormonal mechanisms in aggression, explain why Micah may be having trouble controlling his temper. (16 marks)

Biological explanations of aggression include the role of genetics, neural and hormonal mechanisms and how they are implicated in aggression. Genetic explanations assume that aggression is a hereditary behaviour and that having family members who are aggressive increases your likelihood of being aggressive too. For example, a faulty MAOA gene will interfere with neurochemical activity in the synapse, leading to aggression, so if someone inherits a faulty MAOA gene, aggression is likely. This could explain why Micah is aggressive since he has a family history of aggression. Micah's grandfather has committed a violent crime and is in prison for arson, and Micah's father died whilst in a fight when he was younger. This family history of aggression indicates that Micah's aggression and outbursts at home and school could be inherited and genetic in origin.

Neural and hormonal mechanisms include the role of hormones such as testosterone and regions of the brain such as the limbic system. Testosterone levels correlate with aggression, with many researchers finding that when testosterone levels increase, aggression increases too. Micah may be experiencing an outburst of temper at home and school due to elevated levels of testosterone through puberty or through overproduction. This would explain his outburst and why he has no control over his temper. This also explains why despite her genetic vulnerability, Micah's sisters are calm and easy-going. The sisters may have the same genetic disposition as Micah, but not his levels of testosterone, which is why Micah is experiencing outbursts, yet they are not.

One strength of this explanation is that it has led to various interventions for helping people with aggression. For example, some people with extremely high levels of testosterone can be treated with hormone therapy to help reduce their aggression. In addition, it is also possible to have a surgery called an 'amygdalotomy' where the amygdala is disconnected from the rest of the brain. People who have this surgery experience a loss of emotion, but this includes a loss of aggression. These interventions suggest that this explanation of aggression has been able to contribute to the prevention and reduction of aggression, which may also positively affect crime rates.

One limitation of this explanation of aggression is that it could be considered gender-biased. Many of the studies used to support it are only conducted on male samples. This is beta bias and assumes that the findings from male samples can also be used to explain female aggression and behaviours. This is a limitation because it minimises the differences between men and women and fails to acknowledge differences that would matter. For example, women have higher levels of the hormone oxytocin which means they respond to stress and threats in a very different way than males. Just this one hormonal difference alone suggests that men cannot represent women in aggression research.

One strength of the genetic explanation of aggression is that there is a wealth of research evidence in support of the theory. Godar et al. (2014) used selective breeding to remove the MAOA gene in mice, to see what effect this would have on their behaviour. The mice became more aggressive, and they had disrupted levels of serotonin. They also found that when the mice were given medication to help balance their serotonin levels, the aggressive behaviour stopped. This supports the role of genetics in aggression and the influence that genetics can have on neurotransmitters.

(~575 Words)
Examiner style comments: *Mark band 4*
This is a structured and clear essay which provides a well-detailed account of neural and hormonal causes of aggression while applying the knowledge to Micah. The essay is clear, coherent, and focused. The application is appropriate, and the links to the STEM are explained well.

> Jim was arrested for fighting when watching an England football match. Jim tried justifying himself to the police officer who wrote a note in his notebook. John said: "It wasn't just me, lots of other people were fighting, and some had even run onto the pitch. The referee gave away a penalty to the other team, which was totally not fair; it shouldn't have been a penalty, their played dived. Also, I was with my mates who were the ones who started fighting; I just joined in."

Discuss one or more social psychological explanations for aggression. Refer to some of the comments in the table above in your answer. (16 marks)

One social psychological explanation of aggression is the social learning theory, which assumes that aggression is an acquired behaviour observed in other people. Social learning theory proposes that when we see models performing aggressive behaviour, especially people we admire or identify with, then we are likely to imitate the behaviour too. This can be seen when Jim states that he was 'with mates, who were the ones who started fighting, I just joined in.' This suggests that Jim observed his friends and imitated their behaviour. However, Jim also states that 'it wasn't just me, lots of other people were fighting', which suggests that Jim was also in a psychological state of deindividuation. Deindividuation occurs when we are in crowds such as those found at football matches. This is because being part of a crowd provides anonymity and a loss of self and public awareness. This explains why Jim may have behaved aggressively, even if he normally does not behave this way. Finally, Jim's behaviour could also be explained by the frustration-aggression hypothesis theory, which suggests that when there is frustration that can not be dealt with, the frustration becomes anger. In this case, Jim was frustrated when the 'referee gave away a penalty.' Since there is nothing Jim could have done to change this outcome or alleviate his frustration, he may have turned to aggression to relieve his frustration.

One strength of the deindividuation explanation of aggression is that there is research to support it. Dodd (1985) asked 229 undergraduate psychology students: 'if you could do anything humanly possible with complete assurance that you would not be detected or held responsible, what would you do?' Three independent raters rated the students' responses into those that were antisocial or not. The results found that 36% of the responses were antisocial and 26% were criminal (types of responses referring to acts such as 'robbing a bank'). This research demonstrates the connection between deindividuation as a result of anonymity and subsequent aggression; however, Gerges et al. (1973) found that when eight strangers were placed in a dark room together for an hour with no rules to follow and told that they would never see each other again, it did not take long for talking to cease and for kissing each other to start, suggesting that deindividuation does not inevitably lead to aggression.

One limitation of the frustration-aggression hypothesis is that there is no acknowledgement of other variables that may contribute to the aggression. For example, not everyone who experiences frustration will become aggressive, and not everyone who acts aggressively has done so because of frustration. Berkowitz and Le Page (1967) found that participants behaved more aggressively (delivering electric shocks to others) when they were in the presence of weapons, showing that environmental cues must play a part. In addition, the social learning theory is not able to explain all types of aggression. Whilst it can explain 'proactive' aggression and planned behaviour (for example, where someone has developed the self-efficacy and confidence to repeat aggressive behaviour), it is not able to explain 'reactive' aggression where someone is 'hot headed' or has a reflexive response to a situation or stressor. In this circumstance, there are no predetermined behaviours with rational cognitions and decisions. To explain this type of aggression, a better alternative would be the frustration-aggression hypothesis or a collaboration of both explanations.

(~550 Words)
Examiner style comments: *Mark band 4*
This is a well-detailed and accurate account of social psychological explanations of aggression. The evaluation is well-detailed, thorough, and effective, drawing on a range of points. The use of specialist terminology is excellent. Application to the STEM is effective and accurate.

Aggression	
Cognitive Priming	Cognitive priming refers to a temporary increase in the accessibility of thoughts and ideas, for example, watching aggressive media and using it as a 'script' for your own behaviour.
De-Individuation	The loss of self-awareness that occurs through disguise or being part of a crowd caused by feelings of anonymity.
Desensitisation	The effect on the mind and body when you are repeatedly exposed to aggression and aggressive media, such as a decreased arousal state in the nervous system.
Disinhibition: Aggression	When our normal restraints are loosened after exposure to media violence (e.g. films, TV, video games), aggressive behaviour becomes normalised and is accepted as part of societal behaviour.
Dispositional Explanations: Aggression	Explanations of aggression that focus on the personality or cognitive traits of individuals and how these are the precursors or vulnerabilities to aggression.
Ethological Explanation: Aggression	Explanations of aggression that focus on studies of animal behaviours in their normal habitats to learn about human aggression.
Evolutionary Explanations: Aggression	Explanation of aggression that focuses on how aggressive behaviours and traits may have evolved to enhance our survival and reproduction.
Fixed Action Patterns	A sequence of behaviours that occur in response to a stimulus. For example, an animal may go 'ballistic' in response to a threat.
Frustration-Aggression Hypothesis	Explanation of aggression that assumes that when we are frustrated and unable to find relief or achieve our goals, we become aggressive.
Genetic Factors: Aggression	One biological explanation of aggression that assumes that all aggressive behaviour originates in faulty or mutated genetics. This explanation also assumes that aggressive behaviours are hereditary.
Hormonal Mechanisms: Aggression	A biological assumption that aggression is the result of unbalanced levels or faulty production of hormones such as testosterone. For example, abnormally high levels of testosterone may be correlated with aggression.
Innate Releasing Mechanisms	A physiological, innate process that occurs when triggered by a stimulus. For example, when we interpret something as threatening, an innate releasing mechanism occurs in the brain, which then leads to a fixed action pattern, usually aggression.
Institutional Aggression	Aggression that occurs within a place that is regulated by rules and order, such as prison. For example, institutional aggression in prison may be caused by the prison itself or the traits that prisoners enter with.
Limbic System	A region of the brain that is implicated in regulating mood and behaviour, such as aggression. For example, the hypothalamus is located within the limbic system/area of the brain.
MAOA Gene	A gene that is responsible for producing a chemical that helps neurotransmitters to go through the re-uptake process in the synapse. A fault with the MAOA gene is assumed to be responsible for aggression, according to geneticists and the biological explanation of aggression. For example, low MAOA production could lead to excessive amounts of neurotransmitters in the synapse.
Media Influences: Aggression	Media such as computer games, tv, and films are implicated in aggression. For example, exposure to antisocial and aggressive media is correlated with aggressive behaviours.
Neural Mechanisms: Aggression	Neural mechanisms refer to the role of the brain and biochemistry in the development or cause of aggression. For example, low levels of serotonin are associated with aggressive behaviour.
Serotonin	A neurotransmitter that is implicated in regulating our mood and behaviours through its inhibitory effects on the brain.
Situational Explanations: Aggression	Situational explanations of aggression assume that aggression only occurs because of environmental triggers or stressors within an institution. For example, situational factors in prisons include overcrowding or loss of freedom.
Social Learning Theory: Aggression	Social learning theory assumes that aggression is an acquired behaviour that is learned through observation, imitation and reinforcement, whether this is direct or indirect through the observation of models.

Social Psychological Explanations: Aggression	Explanations of aggression that do not propose that biology is the most dominant cause of aggression. In contrast, social-psychological explanations focus on interactions with each other, the environment or situations.
Testosterone: Aggression	Testosterone is a hormone that is associated with masculinity and aggressive behaviours. For example, high levels of testosterone are correlated with aggression, especially in research where boys enter puberty and exhibit an increase in aggression.

NOTES

NOTES

For more help and support in AQA A-Level Psychology scan the QR code above.

www.tutor2u.net/psychology

AQA | A-Level | Psychology
SKU: 03-4130-30566-03 | ISBN: 978-1915610676